CREDIT REPAIR

AUTHOR : FRANKIE BRACKETT

THE ULTIMATE GUIDE TO IMPROVE YOUR CREDIT REPORT & ACHIEVE CREDIT REPAIR QUICKLY. LEARN THE STRATEGIES & TECHNIQUES OF PROFESSIONAL TO SECURE YOUR PERSONAL FINANCE & FIX YOUR DEBTS

Table of Contents

Introduction 4

Chapter 1.   How to Deal with Bankruptcy 6

Chapter 2.   What Is Credit Repair and How Does It Work? 11

Chapter 3.   Fair Credit Reporting Act Requirements 17

Chapter 4.   What Is Section 609? 23

Chapter 5.   Annual Credit Report 28

Chapter 6.   Look for Errors in the Report 32

Chapter 7.   Credit Scoring and the Automobile Industry 37

Chapter 8.   Properly Dispute Negative Account 42

Chapter 9.   The Truth About Credit Bureaus 48

Chapter 10. How Your Credit Repair Score Is Calculated 54

Chapter 11. The Fico Credit Scores 59

Chapter 12. Simple Steps to Fix Your Credit Scores 64

Chapter 13. Is Credit Repair Ethical? 71

Chapter 14. Why People and Companies Need Credit Repair 77

Chapter 15. Effective Strategies for Repairing Your Credit 81

Chapter 16. Credit Repair Services 86

Chapter 17. Your Financial Freedom 89

Chapter 18. Mindset 92

Conclusion 98

© **Copyright 2021 - All rights reserved.**

The content contained within this book may not be reproduced, duplicated or transmitted without direct written permission from the author or the publisher.

Under no circumstances will any blame or legal responsibility be held against the publisher, or author, for any damages, reparation, or monetary loss due to the information contained within this book. Either directly or indirectly.

Legal Notice:

This book is copyright protected. This book is only for personal use. You cannot amend, distribute, sell, use, quote or paraphrase any part, or the content within this book, without the consent of the author or publisher.

Disclaimer Notice:

Please note the information contained within this document is for educational and entertainment purposes only. All effort has been executed to present accurate, up to date, and reliable, complete information. No warranties of any kind are declared or implied. Readers acknowledge that the author is not engaging in the rendering of legal, financial, medical or professional advice. The content within this book has been derived from various sources. Please consult a licensed professional before attempting any techniques outlined in this book.

By reading this document, the reader agrees that under no circumstances is the author responsible for any losses, direct or indirect, which are incurred as a result of the use of information contained within this document, including, but not limited to, — errors, omissions, or inaccuracies.

Introduction

Credit repair can be very difficult. But by following the steps below, you'll find it's not as hard as you think. The best part is that there are really only three things that matter when it comes to credit repair: understanding your credit score, knowing what items to request for free removal from negative reports, and understanding how much time and money you would save with a cleaned-up credit report."

What exactly is credit repair? It's getting rid of negative information on your credit report that is preventing you from being able to take out loans or get new lines of credit. Some types of this negative information include not paying fees on time or having late payments made by collections agencies. If you have credit repair, you can stop paying late fees and start thinking about taking larger loans with good percentages.

If your credit is bad, it's important to understand how credit scoring works. There are three different explanations of how your credit score is calculated: Fair Isaac, FICO, and Vantage. These three scoring agencies also make up the three main companies that design credit scores. Most creditors will accept all three types of scores. A major factor in choosing a score to use is whether or not the creditor accepts reports from the three agencies. Being aware of which score is most accepted by financial institutions can make a big difference when applying for loans and other types of lines of credit.

Most people start their credit repair by getting negative items removed from their reports. Negative items include collections accounts and late payments made by collection agencies. You have to ask creditors what they charge for removing negative information from your credit report. For example, if they charge onetime fees per item removed, you can pay that amount and then ask them to remove all future negative items free-of-charge whenever you request it at that same time each year in the future. If they charge a yearly fee to remove negative items, you can just pay that amount in the beginning and then request full removal of all future negative items free-of-charge each year at that one time. A one-time charge is offered by some credit repair agencies, although this is not always the best option. Always check with creditors before doing this to make sure you qualify.

Credit repair can be very difficult if you don't understand how your credit score works and what needs to be removed from your credit report if you want new lines of credit. It is important to know what types of negative information are on your credit report and whether or not it's possible for them to remove it. The main thing to remember is that with regard to credit repair, only three things are important: knowing your credit score, knowing the items that need to be removed from negative reports for free, and knowing how much time and money you can save by saving money. Clean up credit reports.

Chapter 1. How to Deal with Bankruptcy

Whether you struggle with debt, are unable to meet all your payments on time, have missed multiple payments on your mortgage or car loan, have maxed out your credit cards, are balancing payments on a number of credit cards to try to keep up to date, or are slipping back on a lot of unsecured debt, the effective bankruptcy option may be what you need to offset your income and debt. If you think the worst possible thing for your credit is bankruptcy, think again. If you're already behind on payments and keep falling further behind or have accounts in collection, bankruptcy may help you start building a strong credit history sooner rather than later.

Before considering how bankruptcy will work for you, you must first familiarize yourself with the various types of bankruptcy, grasp what bankruptcy can and cannot do, and know how it will affect your reputation.

Bankruptcy is the kind of insolvency that most people have heard about. This helps you clear out most consumer debt: credit cards, medical bills, etc. However, in return, you may have to sell some of your properties, such as a second car, expensive electronic equipment, or a holiday home.

Filing for bankruptcy triggers a "complete hold" which automatically prevents most of your creditors from trying to collect what you owe them. Therefore, at least temporarily, creditors can't legally "garnish" (take) your wages; clear your bank account; go after your car, home, or other property; or shut off your services Before your bankruptcy case ends, your past financial issues are in the hands of the bankruptcy court.

A creditor may try to convince you to "reaffirm" (commit to pay off) a debt after your bankruptcy discharge before the insolvency process ends. Once you reassert a loan, think twice. You don't have to reaffirm that debt; if you do, you have to repay it even though all other loans have been paid back. Any arrangement with the bankruptcy court to reassert a loan must be written down and charged. Until the debts are forgiven or within 60 days after the settlement is deposited with the judge, you may void a reassertion deal. If a prosecutor hasn't helped you reach the reaffirmation deal, the court will accept it.

Bankruptcy is not for everybody; it goes without saying. An explanation is that some expenses cannot be washed out of bankruptcy, including:

- Child or spousal care commitments
- Student loans, unless reimbursement will bring you undue hardship (which is very difficult to prove)
- Court-ordered restitution— payments you are ordered to make after a criminal conviction
- Some federal, state, and municipal income taxes longer than three years past due, and any money due.
- Debt on account of death or injury incurred by the intoxicated driving
- Debt on behalf of a marriage settlement agreement or divorce order
- Debt you fail to mention in your bankruptcy documents, unless the claimant hears about your bankruptcy throughout due time.
- Debts the bankruptcy judge regulates were incurred as a result of misconduct on your part — for example, debts incurred as a result of deception (such as lying on a credit application or writing a bad check), malicious harm (such as assault, battery, false imprisonment, libel, or slander), larceny (theft), or breach of confidence or embezzlement.

Not everyone can make use of bankruptcy. Here are some situations when you will not qualify:

- In this case, you earned discharge of your creditors after eight years of filing your new lawsuit (unless you paid 100% of your previously unsecured debts).
- You received debt relief in the case you filed within six years of filing your current 7 cases.
- You have defrauded creditors.

- An earlier bankruptcy lawsuit you brought has been dismissed within the last 180 days because you violated a court order, failed to appear in court as necessary, the court found that your filing was false or represented a misuse of the bankruptcy procedure, or you demanded dismissal after a creditor asked the court to lift the automatic stay.
- The estimated income for a family of your size in the six months before you register is higher than the average income in your state, and you would have enough money left to pay your loans over a five-year term after subtracting all approved expenses. This requirement is referred to as "the test of means," and those who do not pass it may be required to use bankruptcy.

If you have a steady income and think you could squeeze out regular monthly payments. Allows you to keep your property and use your disposable income to pay all or a portion of your debts over three to five years.

You normally have to pay 100 percent of the child support due, for example, but you probably wouldn't have to pay off your credit card debts entirely. To make the bills you can use salaries, bonuses, investment income, business income, or any other money.

Many people file for bankruptcy because they can set up a recovery plan to bring in the new unpaid mortgage or car payments and get back on track for their original loan, to pay off a tax debt without the possibility of foreclosure or repossession.

Nonetheless, these are not the only reasons people file for bankruptcy.

If you cannot fulfill a repayment plan—for example, you lose your job in the scheme for six months and can't make the payments— the bankruptcy court will have the authority to change the program. If the situation seems acute, a grace period, an extended repayment period or a decrease of the total amount due may be offered. If it is clear that due to circumstances beyond your control, you cannot actually fulfill the agreement, the bankruptcy court may even authorize you to discharge (cancel) your debts on the grounds of hardship.

If the bankruptcy court does not authorize you to change your agreement or award you discharge for disability, you have the right to:

- Convert to a bankruptcy
- Dismiss your case if the bankruptcy court won't let you modify your plan or give you a discharge of hardships. A dismissal of your lawsuit will leave you in the same place as before you sued because you owe less due to the contributions you made. The benefit that was withheld from the time you filed the claim until it was rejected will be added to the debt by your creditors.

Bankruptcy and Credit Repair: Does It Help or Hurt?

Bankruptcy is a powerful tool for removing or rising most unsecured debts, and can even cut down on most secured debts— giving you a fresh start. But it will live up to 10 years on your credit report (longer if you apply for a $150,000 or more loan), which is longer than almost any other derogatory thing in your history.

Even though a bankruptcy will lower your credit score immediately, the impact may be smaller than you think.

"Someone who had spotless credit and a very good FICO score might expect a huge decrease in their ratings, according to Fair Isaac.

On the other hand, someone with more derogatory things already reported on their credit report could only see a small decrease in their ratings. "Fair Isaac also warns that the greater the effect on your ranking, the more accounts included in the bankruptcy filing. Doesn't make much of a difference, however— according to Fair Isaac, both have an equally negative effect on your credit score.

Ironically, a bankruptcy will help you start building good credit faster than if you don't file for bankruptcy and keep struggling with more debt than you can afford, particularly if you end up filing bankruptcy again later. Eliminating or eliminating loans by bankruptcy would help you (when the bankruptcy is over) accomplish the two most important goals for a good credit score: meeting your payments on time (35% of your FICO score) and not using the bulk of your available credit (30% of your FICO score). Creditors differ in the way they can offer credit or good interest rates and repayment conditions shortly after a bankruptcy, but they tend to treat the most recent credit issues as more relevant than older problems.

Getting a Mortgage after Bankruptcy

Following one year of interest in a repayment plan, the Federal Housing Administration (FHA) must cover lenders, for two years following discharge. It will consider insuring lenders even more easily following foreclosure, in extenuating circumstances. The FHA needs you to make payments on time and that your interest balances are correct or you don't have new credit commitments after a bankruptcy.

Fannie Mae will not purchase homes if a discharge happened less than two years prior, or a discharge occurred less than four years prior. Private lenders not offering their loans to Fannie Mae may be subject to stricter requirements.

Getting a Credit Card

For many creditors, your sharply reduced debts after bankruptcy and the several-year ban on filing bankruptcy again make you an attractive candidate for credit card offers.

In the past, individuals who filed for bankruptcy, shortly after receiving their bankruptcy discharge, reported receiving several credit cards bids. Banks pulled back on credit card offers during the crisis, but by late 2010, banks were again providing credit cards to people without good credit. Chances are after a foreclosure you'll be able to get credit cards soon. Nonetheless, keep in mind that these cards are expected to carry high-interest rates, annual fees, and other heavy costs.

Chapter 2. What Is Credit Repair and How Does It Work?

Does credit fix truly work? It's an inquiry that has been posed on many occasions by shoppers whose credit score has run into some bad luck and who are prepared to get their budgetary life in the groove again.

Albeit not many of us truly appreciate ads intruding on our favored programming, a large number of us are still surprisingly ready to appreciate an item promotion when it's the superstar — thus, the infomercial. Maybe it's the puzzle, all things considered, since, as a rule, we're left contemplating the item and attempting to choose, "Accomplishes it truly work?!"

Like the mop that vows to clean anything, credit fix can often appear just as it couldn't in any way, shape, or form be the credit report enchantment eraser it's often promoted to be. In any case, hearing the narratives, perusing the surveys, and paging through gathering posts can show blended outcomes, leaving you with that equivalent essential inquiry: "Credits fix truly work?!" In the accompanying book, we'll answer this significant question and give important data on the most proficient method to get your credit score back to a decent number.

Indeed, So Long as Your Items Qualify for Dispute

With everything taken into account, the response to the subject of whether credit fix works is a lot of a run of the mill, "Truly, however... "Yes, credit fix can work to expel certain negative things from your credit reports. Be that as it may, it doesn't work for each kind of thing — and it unquestionably isn't a prompt, enchantment credit score sponsor.

Basically, credit fix is the way toward questioning things on your credit report that are an out-of-line or wrong portrayal of your monetary history. The capacity to record credit report questions is given to assist you with guaranteeing your credit report isn't brimming with bogus information that can be utilized against you in loaning choices.

If you identify data in your document that is deficient or mistaken, and report it to the purchaser detailing the organization, the office must research except if your debate is trivial.
— FTC

What credit fix isn't is a simple method to expel genuinely earned critical credit report marks or an approach to discard real obligations. Not exclusively are these debates liable to be dismissed, yet the credit departments don't have to research questions that are viewed as negligible.

The Most Likely to Be Successfully Disputed Items

The most ideal approach to have credit fix achievement is to realize what's in store from the procedure before you begin. If you go into it with an expanded feeling of what you'll achieve, you'll clearly be baffled at long last. Reasonable desires can go far in credit fix (and money when all is said in done).

Along these lines, it boils down to knowing which things on your credit report really meet the qualifications for a fruitful debate.

Since the procedure is intended to guarantee your reports are exact, the sorts of things that can ordinarily be expelled through credit fix are those that are, well, off base here and there. This incorporates things that are wrong, false, obsolete, or unverified.

Mistaken Items

The least demanding kind of thing to contest is one that is only completely incorrect. This spreads fundamental blunders, such as spelling botches or distorted sums that can create turmoil or credit issues. For instance, if that decimal point is in an inappropriate spot, it might seem as though you have unquestionably more obligation than you should. Much of the time, basic slip-ups require little exertion for the credit department to explore and can be fixed in a genuinely short measure of time.

Obsolete Items

Another sort of questionable thing that is commonly simple to fix are things that are obsolete. Most negative things can just stay on your credit report for a set measure of time before they should be expelled. Hard credit requests, for example, last as long as two years, while reprobate installments can last up to seven. When these things hit their maximum age, be that as it may, they ought to be expelled from your report consequently or you can record a debate to have them evacuated.

Fake Items

If you've at any point been the survivor of data fraud, you could end up with fake records on your credit reports. While these records may appear to be authentic from the outset, further examination can often disclose their vile birthplaces. Notwithstanding documenting debates to have fake records expelled from your reports, make certain to report any instances of fraud immediately.

Unconfirmed Items

The remainder of the as often as possible contested things are those records on your reports that can't be validated by the data suppliers. If they can't show that the obligation or deprecatory imprint truly has a place with you, the credit departments will evacuate the thing.

When considering a credit fix, make certain to check each of the three of your credit reports. Credit authorities depend on outsiders to report your money-related conduct, so few out of every odd thing is accounted for to each of the three buyer credit departments (Equifax, Experian, and TransUnion).

Thus, a couple of your credit reports could house questionable things that don't appear on different reports. Since you can't foresee which credit report(s) a creditor will use to decide your credit hazard, every one of the three of your reports ought to be in acceptable condition to forestall passing up credit later on.

The Top Credit Repair Companies

Similarly, as with numerous things in life, credit fix is a procedure that you can do yourself — or you can recruit an expert. The course you take will rely for the most part upon you (and your credit reports). If your credit report questions are basic and clear, for example, a spelling mistake or obsolete thing, then documenting yourself might be quick and simple.

If your questions are increasingly included, in any case, it might be less upsetting to employ an accomplished credit fix organization to follow up for your benefit. This can be especially obvious in situations where you have to introduce significant proof to back up your debate. A portion of our top-of-the-line credit fix organizations has many years of experience helping purchasers expel things from their credit reports.

Most credit fix organizations will work under a month-to-month expense, which is charged for every month that they chip away at your sake. Credit fix is once in a while a brisk procedure, so be set up to pay for the administration for at any rate a couple of months if you go that course. Convoluted credit fix cases including different debates may take a half year or more to get results.

One thing to note is that credit fix organizations can't lawfully ensure positive outcomes (at any rate, not in such a significant number of words). If a credit correction organization guarantees that you will see a specific number of things thrown out of their reports, you may need to take a closer look at the organization's visibility, or just make another decision.

How the Credit Repair Process Works

Contesting wrong things on your credit report is a legitimate right allowed to you by the Fair Credit Reporting Act (FCRA), which secures your entitlement to reasonable and precise credit reports.

While debates once should have been submitted recorded as a hard copy through the mail, even the credit authorities have modernized to where you can document most questions online through the department's site. By all accounts, credit fix seems like a straightforward procedure. What's more, it very well maybe. "Be that as it may, " The multifaceted nature of the procedure will in general change with the idea of your debates.

To begin, a different question should be petitioned for everything and for each credit report. This implies you'll require three individual debates to evacuate a solitary thing that shows up on every one of the three reports, which should be finished by composing letters to every department or visiting every authority's site.

When you present your debate, you should make certain to incorporate the same number of supporting or potentially evidentiary reports as you can. Continuously submit duplicates with your question, never present your unique reports.

You'll additionally need to keep a duplicate of your contest and any correspondence identified with it — just on the off chance that an issue emerges.

When a contest is gotten by the agency, it has 30 days to examine the thing being referred to and react to your debate. Some portion of this prerequisite is that the organization should advance your debate and any data you give to the gathering that gave the data.

The data supplier should then explore the thing being referred to, looking into all applicable data and announcing the outcomes to the credit agency. If the data furnisher sees the thing as off base, it is required to notify every one of the three credit departments and solicitation that the thing be expelled from the entirety of your credit reports.

After the examination, the authority is required to illuminate you regarding the outcomes recorded as a hard copy, alongside a duplicate of your report if things were adjusted. You can likewise demand the announcing organization to send notification of these amendments to any individual who has gotten your credit report in the previous half-year.

Fix the Root of Your Credit Problems for Lasting Success

While the late-night infomercial might be as much about the promoting as the "stunning" items it highlights, it unquestionably doesn't lessen the feeling of the puzzle that originates from thinking about whether that little device truly is the wonder they portray it. Be that as it may, even apparently innocuous infomercials can turn grievous for the individuals who genuinely need whatever contraption they're selling to really work.

For some, shoppers, a credit fix can from the start appear to be a simple method to clean away the credit harm holding down their credit scores. Shockingly, credit fix is one item that doesn't "do everything" — paying little heed to how it's occasionally publicized.

While this shouldn't imply that credit fix doesn't work — it does, give your contested things meet the necessities — however, it positively isn't a fix-all. The most ideal approach to guarantee enduring credit achievement is to address the issues that made you search out credit fix in any case.

Chapter 3. Fair Credit Reporting Act Requirements

The federal law governing credit reporting is the Fair Credit Reporting Act (FCRA).

Congress enacted the FCRA in 1970 to give consumers more control over what information goes into their credit history.

The FCRA sets limits on who can access consumer credit reports, how their information is used, and how long it stays on file. It also provides for an avenue of recourse if a person believes that inaccurate information has been reported.

If you have questions about the requirements of the FCRA or need assistance with any aspect thereof, please contact our experienced attorneys for a consultation.

Legislative History

The Fair Credit Reporting Act (FCRA), Pub. L. No. 90-321, 82 Stat. 168 (1966), codified at 15 U.S.C. § 1681 et seq., was enacted by Congress on October 27, 1970, in response to government surveys which revealed widespread inaccurate information reported by consumer reporting agencies about the personal histories of consumers. The Act "was designed to revise the practices of such agencies by limiting their access to certain records" and "to review the accuracy of their reports." Although it is not a criminal statute, it significantly changed the practices of many federal and state agencies that previously had access to credit reports without limits.

The Act is codified at 15 U.S.C. § 1681-1681q, and became effective on October 20, 1971. Among other things, the FCRA requires consumer reporting agencies to maintain reasonable procedures for verifying the accuracy of the information concerning consumers that they furnish to third parties and establishes procedures under which consumers may dispute the accuracy of such information.

The FCRA confers broad powers upon both federal and state regulatory agencies. The Act establishes a Federal Trade Commission (FTC) Bureau of Consumer Protection to administer and enforce its provisions directly or through delegation to other appropriate federal or state agencies. Each agency designated by the FTC has primary enforcement responsibility with respect to particular types of entities. For example, the FTC designates the Federal Reserve Board as the agency responsible for administering and enforcing the Act's requirements regarding consumer reports that are used or disseminated by banks.

The Act authorizes other federal agencies to enforce compliance with its requirements. The U.S. Postal Service, for example, is authorized by 15 U.S.C. § 1681s-2 to enforce compliance with certain requirements of the FCRA with respect to consumer reports relating to credit transactions involving the mail. The Federal Trade Commission, in turn, shares enforcement authority over the same provisions with state attorneys general under 15 U.S.C. § 1681s-6.

The FCRA also imposes certain conditions on certain types of business entities. For example, an insurance company must comply with the FCRA if it furnishes a consumer report to a person who is seeking to obtain credit. It also imposes requirements on banks with respect to deposit holding companies and their affiliates.

Personal Information

Certain kinds of personal information are excluded from the Act's scope. It does not apply to information regarding tenancies of real estate that is used for no purpose other than to enable the owner to collect the rent or to protect the premises. The Act's requirements do not apply to information relating to securities or commodities transactions, nor does it cover any "consumer report [that] contains any ... credit score or any other risk score or predictability indicator

There are two exceptions to the prohibition against obtaining credit reports without prior written notice. The Fair Credit Reporting Act does not apply to "the communication of a credit report by any person to whom such report is communicated in accordance with the standardized Mortgage Data Bank System of Department of Housing and Urban development. "Also, the FCRA does not apply when a person "furnishes information to a consumer reporting agency regarding any inquiry made by such person for use in determining the propriety of granting credit to an individual."

Consumer Reports

Any written, oral, or other contact by a consumer reporting agency that provides information about a consumer's creditworthiness, credit status, or creditworthiness is called a consumer report (also known as a background check). This includes a consumer's credit history and any information that is compiled using any of the information in a credit report.

Consumer Reporting Agencies

A consumer reporting agency (CRA) is defined as any person who regularly engages in assembling or evaluating consumer credit information or other information on consumers for the purpose of furnishing consumer reports to third parties. The definition specifically excludes persons who assemble or evaluate consumer credit information only for the purposes of "applications for, or operation of, a person's business by which loans are originated" and "debt collecting activities under [the Fair Debt Collection Practices Act] ... [and] insurance activities... in connection with insurance issued by persons other than such creditors.

Consumer reporting agencies are subject to a number of requirements contained in the Fair Credit Reporting Act. Among them is a requirement to regularly review their files on consumers to identify information that is inaccurate, obsolete, or of insufficient importance to warrant keeping, and remove that information. The information must be removed when it is more than seven years old in the case of adverse actions and more than six months old for bankruptcy filings. The FCRA also requires consumer reporting agencies to keep, for at least five years, written records regarding consumer complaints received by them.

Consumer reports may be obtained by employers during the pre-employment process. It does not require an employer to obtain a consumer report on an individual it is considering hiring, however; additional requirements may apply in that situation.

The FCRA's obligations apply only to consumer reporting agencies that "regularly" provide credit reports. This is defined as at least one credit report per month for each consumer whose credit information is in their files, and at least 20 or more such reports in any year. A single "credit report" may be composed of various information from different sources; for example, a single report might summarize all the information contained in three credit reports. The FCRA sets up a national system of self-regulation for consumer reporting agencies. Consumer reporting agencies are subject to periodic examination by the Federal Trade Commission (FTC) and must meet minimum standards that are set up by the FTC. Consumer reporting agencies may not charge consumers fees for placing, removing, or correcting information in their reports; however, a consumer reporting agency may charge its regular and reasonable fees to describe its services and any additional information it provides upon request. The maximum amount that a consumer reporting agency may charge for providing copies of records is $12.50 per consumer report. There are additional rules governing the sale of information obtained from a credit report in connection with the sale of goods or services.

Consumer reporting agencies have been under scrutiny and criticism lately for their business practices, as they have become powerful corporations and an increasingly important part of the economy. The changing economic market has meant that consumer reports are getting more detailed and complicated, but federal guidelines mean that only so much information can be included in any given credit report. The issue remains that, despite these legally imposed restrictions, a credit report may contain information that is not accurate, and there have been instances of identity theft as a result. Also, because the existing federal regulations are not made binding on states with respect to consumer reporting agencies located in their jurisdictions, major state governments have had to enact similar laws governing consumer reporting agencies.

The Fair Credit Reporting Act (FCRA) is enforced by the Federal Trade Commission (FTC). The FTC has an established complaint procedure for consumers and businesses affected by credit reports. Additionally, the FTC or private citizens also can bring lawsuits against credit bureaus that wrongfully deny consumers access to their reports or fail to correct errors in their reports.

History

The Federal Trade Commission (FTC) began examining the use of credit information in consumer reports as early as the 1950s. In 1973, the FTC held the first public hearings on pre-employment credit checks, and in 1974, the Commission held hearings about unfair and deceptive practices in the sale of credit reports. In 1977, Congress authorized federal agencies to investigate "unfair or deceptive acts or practices" by consumer reporting agencies. The FCRA was enacted in response to these investigations.

The Act establishes a Bureau of Consumer Protection within the Federal Trade Commission (FTC) to administer and enforce its provisions. The Bureau is required to perform investigations and audits and to issue reports of its activities. The FTC also has the power to bring civil actions to enforce compliance with the Act, as well as the ability to obtain injunctions and assess civil penalties.

Credit reporting agencies are subject to a number of requirements contained in the FCRA. Among them is a requirement that they regularly review their files on consumers to identify information that may be inaccurate, obsolete, or of insufficient importance or value to warrant keeping. Credit reporting agencies must make reasonable efforts to notify consumers when information is removed from a consumer report because it does not meet the criteria for inclusion. In addition, agencies must maintain a toll-free telephone number to allow consumers to get additional information about their reports, and to challenge information that they believe is inaccurate. They also must not charge consumers fees for placing, removing, or correcting information in the consumer's report.

Credit reporting agencies are prohibited from taking adverse action against any consumer because of any inquiry concerning a consumer's creditworthiness, credit standing, or credit capacity that was made by or on behalf of the consumer. Credit reporting agencies must make a consumer report available to anyone who is authorized to obtain the consumer report. They may not sell or rent information about consumers to a third party unless the information is aggregated or de-identified.

Credit bureaus and "consumer reporting agencies" are prohibited from including any derogatory information about an individual in a consumer report if they know the information is false, or if they have reasonable grounds to believe it is false. The Federal Trade Commission has published detailed guidelines as well as fact sheets on its website explaining how these rules apply in specific situations. For example, the FTC states that a "credit check typically includes information from various sources. The credit report includes information from the consumer's credit history and financial obligations. Information about the consumer's employment, assets, debts, income and taxes is obtained by contacting the employer of the consumer and other individuals who know about the consumer."

Consumer reporting agencies must provide consumers with some types of free reports for up to three years. They also must make certain disclosures regarding their policies for providing reports to third parties. For example, they must let consumers know if they are restricting access to their reports or if they will be sharing information with a third party (including employers or insurance companies) without obtaining advance consent. The agency also must provide consumers with information about whether the agency uses a consumer's credit report as part of its decision-making process, and explain how the agency obtains and uses this information.

Congress set up some rules for how consumer reporting agencies operate that apply only to those agencies located in different states from the state where the consumer lives. For example, if a consumer lives in New York but his or her credit report is maintained by a company based in Florida, that company must comply with New York state laws.

Chapter 4. What Is Section 609?

A 609 is known as a dispute letter, which you would send to your creditor if you saw you were overcharged or unfairly charged. Most people use a 609 letter in order to get the information they feel they should have received. There are several reasons why some information might be kept from you.

A section 609 letter is sent after two main steps. First, you see that the dispute is on your credit report. Second, you have already filed and processed a debt validation letter. The basis of the letter is that you will use it in order to take unfair charges off your credit report, which will then increase your credit score.

The 609 letters can easily help you delete your bad credit. Other than this, there are a couple of other benefits you will receive from the letter. One of these benefits is that you will obtain your documentation and information as the credit bureau has to release this information to you. Secondly, you will be able to obtain an accurate credit report, which can definitely help you increase your credit score.

There are also disadvantages to the 609 letters. One of these disadvantages is that collection agencies can add information to your credit history at any time. A second disadvantage is that you still have to repay debt. You cannot use the 609 letters in order to remove the debt that you are obligated to pay. Finally, your creditor can do their investigation and add the information back into your credit report, even if it was removed (Irby, 2019).

One of the reasons section 609 came to be is because one of five people state they have inaccurate information on the credit report (Black, 2019). At the same time, many people believe that this statistic is actually higher than 20 percent of Americans.

How Section 609 Works to Repair Bad Credit

If you notice anything on your report that should not be there, you need to use the section 609 loophole in order to file a dispute, which could result in their wrong information being taken off of the report. If this is the case, your credit score will increase, as you will no longer have this negative inaccuracy affecting your score.

How to File a Dispute with Section 609

It is important to note that there are several template letters for section 609. This means you can quickly and easily download and use one of these models. While you usually have to pay for them, there are some for free. Of course, you must remember to include your information in the letter before you send it.

You should make sure all the procedure is done correctly, as this will make it more likely that the information will come off and no one will place it back on your report again.

1. Find a dispute letter through googling "section 609 dispute letters." While you might be able to find a free download, for some, you will be able to copy and paste into Microsoft Word or onto a Google Doc.
2. Make the necessary changes to the letter. This will include changing the name and address. You must also make sure your phone number is included. Sometimes people include the email address, but this is not necessary. In fact, it is always safer to only include your home address or PO Box information. You must also check the whole letter. If something does not match what you want to say, such as what you are trying to dispute on your credit report, you need to state this. These letters are quite generic, which means you need to add in your information.
3. Make sure that all of the account information you want to be taken off your credit report is handwritten. Likewise, we recommend you use blue ink rather than black. On top of this, you do not need to worry about being too neat, but make sure they can read the letters and numbers correctly. This is an important part of filing your dispute letter because handwritten ones in blue ink will not be pushed through their automated system. They have an automatic system that will read the letter for them and punch in the account number you use. They will then send you a generic letter that states these accounts are now off your credit report, which does not mean that it

actually happened. When you write the information down, a person needs to read it and will typically take care of it. Of course, there's always the chance that you'll be ignored. Unfortunately, this can happen with any letters.

4. You must prove who you are with your letters. While this is never a comfortable thing to do, you must send a copy of your social security card and your driver's license or they will shred your letter. You also need to make sure that you get each of your letters notarized. You will usually do this by going to the courthouse in your district.

5. You can send as many letters as you need; however, keep in mind that the creditor typically will not make you send more than four. This is because when you threaten to take them to court in the third letter, they will realize that your accounts and demands just are not worth it. First, you could damage their reputation, and secondly, you will cost them more money than simply taking the information off your credit report will.

6. It is necessary to keep all correspondence they send you. When they try to force you to submit more information or keep telling you that they can't do something, this will come in handy. It is important that you do not surrender. Many people struggle to get them to pay attention because that is just how the system works. Therefore, you should not listen to their quick automatic reply that your information is off your credit report. You should also wait at least three months and then re-run your credit report to make sure the wrong information has been removed. Keep track of every time you need to re-run your credit report as you can use this as proof if they continue to send you a letter stating the information is off of your credit report.

It is important to note that you can now file a dispute letter online with all three credit bureaus. However, this is a new system, which means that it does come with more problems than sending one through the mail. While it is completely your choice whether you use a form to file your 609 dispute or send a letter, you should always keep copies and continue to track them, even if you don't hear from the credit bureau after a couple of months. It will never hurt to send them a second letter or even a third.

What Are My Rights Under 609?

The Fair Credit Reporting Act is going to cover many of the aspects and the components of credit checking to make sure that it is able to maintain a reasonable amount of privacy and accuracy along the way. This agency is going to list all of the responsibilities that credit reporting companies and any credit bureaus will have, and it includes the rights of the consumer that will be your rights in this situation. This Act is going to be the part that will govern how everything is going to work to ensure that all parties are treated in a fair manner.

When using this act, the consumer has to be told if any of the information on your file has been in the past or is now being used against you in any way, shape, or form. You have a right to know whether the information is harming you and what that information is.

In addition, the consumer is going to have the right to go through and dispute any information that may be seen as inaccurate or incomplete at the time. If they see that there are items in the documents they are sent, if the billing to them is not right or there is something else off in the process, the consumer has the right to dispute this and the credit reporting agency needs to at least look into it and determine if the consumer is right.

This Act is going to limit the access that third parties can have to your file. You personally have to go through and provide your consent before someone is able to go through and look at your credit score, whether it is a potential employer or another institution providing you with funding.

They are not able to get in and just look at it. Keep in mind that if you do not agree for them to take a look at the information, it is going to likely result in you not getting the funding that you want, because there are very few ways that the institution can fairly assess the risk that you pose to them in terms of creditworthiness.

It means that you may have debt or another negative item on your credit report, but there is a way to get around this without having to wait for years to get that to drop off your report or having to pay back a debt that you are not able to afford.

Keep in mind that this is not meant to be a method for you to take on many debts that you cannot afford and then just dump them. But on occasion, there could be a few that you are able to fight and get an instant boost to your credit score in the process.

Why Use a 609 Letter?

The 609 Letter is going to be one of the newest credit repair secrets that will help you remove a lot of information on your credit report, all of the false information, and sometimes even the accurate information, thanks to a little loophole found in our credit reporting laws. You can use this kind of letter in order to resolve some of the inaccuracies that show up, to dispute your errors, and handle some of the other items that could inaccurately come in and impact and lower your credit score.

Using these 609 letters is a good way for us to clean up our credit a bit and in some cases, it is going to make a perfect situation. However, we have to remember that outside of some of the obvious benefits that we are going to discuss, there are a few things that we need to be aware of ahead of time.

There are few limitations that are going to come with this as well. For example, even after you work with the 609 letters, it is possible that any information considered as accurate could be added to the report again, even after the removal. This is going to happen if the creditor is able to verify the accuracy. They may take it off for a bit if the 30 days have passed and they are not able to verify at that point. But if the information is accurate, remember that it could end up back on the report.

Chapter 5.   Annual Credit Report

An annual credit report is a free service that lets you see what details credit reporting agencies to have on you. This is a valuable thing to do every year to make sure your report is accurate and up-to-date.

Discovering inaccuracies on your credit report can be difficult, as it may not be easy or possible for you to find them on your own. There are many companies that offer this service for a fee but it's best to check with the agencies first before paying someone else because they may charge more than necessary or provide less information than they would otherwise if you contacted them directly.

In some cases, the company will offer services similar in function as those offered by AnnualCreditReport.com, which does not itself release any credit report information to the public. The company may also ask you to sign an agreement that states you won't release the information to anyone else, but these agreements are often reversed by court order and are therefore unenforceable.

Annual Credit Report: What You Need to Know

Nobody wants a low credit score. That said, there are a lot of things that people don't know about their credit report and how it affects their scores more than they realize. One of those crucial tidbits that most people don't know is that they can purchase an annual credit report and see for themselves what is going on with their own personal finances.

Understanding the Annual Credit Report

The truth is that most people have no idea what an annual credit report is, and some may think it's a scam. It is not a scam, although there are some who will try to make a quick buck by offering you something that has no real value for you. But if you understand the basics of your credit report and what truly goes into it, then you will be more likely to realize when something you get in the mail from an unknown source is not worth your time or money.

Did You Know? People can purchase their own credit reports once every 12 months for free. Federal law mandates that everyone's credit report be available to them on request, and this is what an annual credit report is. The free report is expected to contain all of the specifics of your personal credit history from Equifax, Experian, and TransUnion, the three main credit bureaus.

What Does an Annual Credit Report Contain?

The annual credit report includes everything that is in your current credit report including:

- When was the last time you demanded to see a sample of your own work?
- The length of time each account has been open and how long it's been since you have updated any information on it.
- The accounts that you have listed as public records
- The accounts that you have listed as paid collections.
- What goes on with the accounts you have listed as bad credit loans.

There are other details of your credit report that will be included in your annual credit report, and it is up to you to thoroughly look over the information and make sure it's an accurate representation of what is in your credit report. If there are mistakes, then you must contact the appropriate agency or company immediately so they can fix the problem. Although it might not seem to be a major issue, even a minor mistake on your credit report can cause problems when applying for a loan. Some credit reporting agencies are not required to fix mistakes, so you could find yourself having to pay for a service you do not need.

Why It's Important for You to Know about Your Credit Report

A good credit score is a key ingredient in people who want to access loans, and it may seem like the best way to get a good credit score is to just keep on paying off debt until there isn't any left at all. This is an excellent example of how money can lead to problems, and you can avoid falling into the same pit.

You should check your credit report to see how much of your debt is due to loans. For example, if you're carrying a balance on just one or two credit cards, then it can be very easy to pay them off. The problem is that those balances will remain in your report and not appear to you as paid off. There are other accounts that can accumulate over time, like medical bills or even public record debts like tax liens. It's best to research the good and bad in every account before you go into debt if you want to have a better understanding of what's on your credit report and know what problems could arise down the road if there are mistakes in your report.

Getting a free copy of your credit report might seem like a waste of time, but you will be able to get an accurate sense of what's on your report and how it's affecting your current credit rating. It's also a good idea to double-check that anything in your current report is right, so you can contact the appropriate agencies if anything is missing or wrong.

What Is the Best Way to Get a Copy of Your Credit Report?

The process for getting a copy of your own credit report varies from state to state and can be different in other countries as well. You can find some great tips for how to get access to your own credit report here. But in a nutshell, it's as simple as going to the credit bureau website and requesting a copy of your credit report.

The site will tell you where to send the information or you can go ahead and email them directly. If you're feeling a little overwhelmed, then send everything at once and make sure to check everything for accuracy. If anything is in error, then you should contact the appropriate company immediately so they can look into it.

What Is an Annual Credit Report Worth?

The obvious question is: does an annual credit report have any real value? The answer in most cases is no, and this is because you do not need to see your own annual report every year. In fact, it might be better to wait a few years until you really need to access your report and look at the information. By then you can get a clearer picture of your credit history and see if there are any errors in your report or if there is anything you can do to fix them.

It's important to realize that more than likely you will not have any new debt or credit cards added to your report, so there is little reason for you to get a copy every year. The only time you should request an annual credit report is if something doesn't seem quite right about the information in your current report. If you get a bad score, then you want to investigate the reason why. It could be that there is some inaccurate information on your report or someone else's report with your same name listed as a previous address. If you have ever been involved in identity theft before, then this may be an important step in keeping your personal information safe and secure. Anytime you look at your credit report, make sure that the company is giving you a free copy and not charging for it.

Other good ways to find out how good your credit is and what problems you might face in the future are available as well. You will find more information on that topic in our guide. In short, you'll want to make sure your credit score is as good as possible if you want to take advantage of the many great offers available and maintain financial power.

Chapter 6. Look for Errors in the Report

You need to eliminate all harmful credit report errors and inaccuracies from all three credit bureaus. The U.S. Public Interest Research Group (PIRG), an advocacy group, released a survey indicating that seven out of every ten credit reports contained some kind of error or mistake. The survey also found one out of every four credit reports had errors considered serious enough to prevent a borrower from getting a loan or credit. This survey shows we need to actively make sure our credit report is accurate. You are working hard to build your credit, do not allow other people's errors to negatively affect you...To hinder your hard work and earned rewards.

Every credit report is built on information gathered, purchased, and/or reported by creditors and third-party groups. If false or inaccurate information has made it to your credit report, then your credit report will reflect this false or inaccurate information. False or inaccurate information on your credit report can damage your credit, and cause you to pay higher interest rates, credit fees, and loan costs, or even prevent you from obtaining loans.

The sooner you identify harmful errors or inaccuracies in your credit report and work with your creditor and credit bureau to correct them, the sooner your credit score will improve. However, not all errors and inaccuracies are harmful.

1. Credit scenario: a revolving credit account (such as a credit card) was opened over 12 months ago, the credit limit is $1,000.00, the balance owed is three hundred dollars or less, and all monthly payments have been made on time.
2. Not harmful: any increase to your credit history or your credit limit only helps your credit and should not be corrected.
3. Harmful: any decrease made to your credit history, either to your credit limit or the report of any late payments, is harmful and should be corrected as soon as possible.

- Credit experts recommend individuals review their credit reports at least once every 12 months for harmful inaccuracies and errors. Data on how to order free credit reports are found below.
- It is important to verify the accuracy of dates, especially on every negative credit report. Bankruptcy, foreclosures, repossessions, late payments, and other negative credit information begin losing their negative effect after twelve months. Reviewing your credit report for accurate dates allows you to get rid of past negative events sooner.
- Check for indications you have been a victim of identity fraud. Search your report for names, social security numbers, and accounts that are not yours.

NOTE: some creditors "re-age" debt. This means a creditor may report negative information like bankruptcy, foreclosure, judgment, or collections as recently as today, as opposed to the true date. Re-aging is done for many reasons, from a simple reporting error to full manipulation by the creditor with the purpose of selling the "fresh debt" to debt collectors. Re-aging negative reports are something you need to be on the lookout for because it will significantly hurt your credit. If you find negative information has been re-aged, immediately work with that creditor and credit bureau to correct the error.

Credit Report Errors

The credit report is the key to building and improving your credit score. The quicker you build credit and show a strong twelve months of credit history, the quicker you can improve your credit score. However, excessive credit use, late or non-payments, and errors all hurt your credit score.

A credit report error can be as simple as having a repeated or duplicated collection account, wrong address, or wrong account name. Credit report errors can include reduced or missing credit limits, inflated credit balances, debts belonging to other people, multiple social security numbers, wrong addresses, and wrong or incorrect variations on your name.

Simply speaking, you can combine most credit errors into two groups: high priority and low priority credit errors. Since all credit scores are based solely on the credit report, removing high-priority errors will result in the quickest and most permanent improvements.

High-priority credit errors include inaccurate reporting of credit limits and balances owed. In order to build and strengthen your credit, it is important to show as high a credit limit as possible, with a balanced owed of no more than 30% of the credit limit. Other high-priority credit errors include an old bankruptcy being reported as filed within the last year.

Low priority credit errors include inaccurate reporting of irrelevant or helpful factors. Exaggerated credit limits will not hurt you. Repossession of an auto ten years ago, being reported as occurring eight years ago will not hurt your credit. Do not correct errors that are in your favor. Low-priority credit errors are not likely to hurt your credit score and can be ignored. Focus your time and resources on correcting high-priority negative errors.

High-Priority Credit Report Errors
- Collection notices are listed more than once (duplicates).
- Mistakes or errors in your payment history that occurred within the past two years.
- Missing or reduced account credit limits.
- Collection notices that are not yours.
- Incorrect information such as a current address, prior addresses, and current employer.
- Accounts that do not belong to you (this could indicate identity fraud or the beginning of your credit report is merged with another person's report).
- Someone else's social security number or a mistake in your social security number (this could indicate identity fraud or the beginning of your credit report is merged with another person's report).
- Someone else's name or a mistake in your name (this could indicate identity fraud or the beginning of your credit report being merged with another person's report).

Low-Priority Credit Report Errors

- Mistakes in your payment history that occurred more than two years ago.
- Delinquencies were older than seven years.
- Beneficial account inaccuracies (e.g., inflated credit limits).
- The wrong date of birth is a low priority error—unless you think you might be a victim of identity fraud.
- Typos in account numbers are a low priority—unless you believe you might be a victim of identity fraud.

Disputing Credit Report Errors

After reviewing each credit report, you find a high-priority credit error—what's next? You need to take action and get those errors deleted or corrected as quickly as possible. Begin by writing the offending credit bureau and the creditor directly. See the appendix called "credit dispute letter" for an example of a dispute letter, and the appendix called "how to get your free credit report" and "identity theft: how to report it" for credit bureau contact information. Be sure your letter specifies the error and be specific in how the error needs to be corrected, and request a letter confirming the action taken to be mailed to you.

Disputing an error with a credit bureau or creditor is free. Once you formally contact them, they will investigate the disputed claim and, if applicable, delete or correct the error. The following three steps are recommended when disputing an error with the credit bureaus:

Step One: Contact the Offending Credit Bureau

- It is possible that not all creditors report to all the credit bureaus. For this reason, only contact the credit bureau(s) that is reporting the erroneous negative credit information.
- Use the "credit report dispute letter—sample" found in the appendix.
- Explain in your letter what is inaccurate and give specific directions as to the corrective action you want to be taken.

- When possible, include proof in your letter to support the claim.
- Enclose a copy of the credit report, with the item(s) in question circled. (Make sure to send the credit report to the corresponding credit bureau.)
- The credit bureau is required to confirm with the creditor and investigate the disputed information within 30 days.
- The creditor is required by law to investigate the disputed data and report its findings.
- If the dispute results in a change to your credit report, the credit bureau will send you a written response and a free copy of your updated credit report.
- However, if the creditor disagrees with your claim, the credit bureau will mail you a written explanation stating the disputed item is accurate.

Step Two: Keep a Record

- Keep records of all phone and email communications.
- Keep copies of every letter sent and received.
- Keep proof supporting your claim—this can include anything from canceled payment checks to past billing statements.
- If you're missing key billing statements, the Fair Credit Billing Act requires each creditor to keep past statements on file which you can request for a fee.
- Call the billing or creditor registration department and ask what you need.

Step Three: Keep at It

Continue to check your credit reports once a year at the very least. Make sure no new derogatory or harmful errors or negative information has been added to your credit report, and the corrected errors have not been included in your credit record.

NOTE: you are not alone in this fight. As of 2012, you can now ask the federal government to help you fix credit report errors.

Chapter 7.   Credit Scoring and the Automobile Industry

Over the past few years, credit scoring has become a central part of the automotive industry. It was adopted as a standard way to determine if potential car buyers should be approved for loans or not. Currently, there is much contention and debate over this method.

Credit scoring is a system that assigns risk scores to individuals based on their past credit history. These scores are used to help banks or other lenders decide whether the individual should be approved for a loan, thus allowing them to charge higher interest rates when they need to. In order to understand how credit scoring works and what it has done for the automobile industry, one must first understand risk analysis.

Risk analysis is often used in business settings where there are many different variables that contribute towards an outcome like financial loss or success. For example, if a car were to be manufactured at a loss and sold, the manufacturer could lose a significant amount of money. If the manufacturer sells 100 cars for $5000 each but loses $500 on each car sold, they would incur a $50 000 loss for selling those 100 cars. However, if the cars were to be manufactured at a profit and sold for $10000 each, then the net profit would be around $50000.

Credit scoring is based on risk analysis in that it is used in order to determine how risky it would be to give someone credit. The more information a bank can gather about an individual, the more accurate their risk analysis can be. This is why credit scoring is useful because it can dramatically help inform lenders so they can make more informed loan decisions.

Credit scoring has become a method of measuring risk in almost every business sector as well as every industry (e.g., the automotive industry). While the majority of businesses will only utilize credit scoring systems in the financial sector, there are still many businesses that utilize credit scoring systems outside of their financial sector. For example, insurance agencies may use this system to decide whether or not individuals should be insured or how much an individual should pay depending on their insurance policy. Credit scoring affects the automobile industry in that if policyholders are considered at a high risk of defaulting on their payments, the interest rate will be increased. This is why credit scoring is so important to the auto industry.

How Credit Scoring Works

Credit score is made up of different numbers that are determined by using the information as well as factors of your personal life such as income, debt, housing status/amount you owe on your mortgage, length of time since you last paid on an outstanding balance, etc. It is all part of a complex process that lenders use to determine if they should approve or decline your request for a loan.

The Automobile Industry

In order to understand how credit scoring works and what it has done for the automobile industry, one must first understand risk analysis. In the past, car dealerships were just as susceptible to financial loss as a manufacturer losing money selling a car. However, with credit scoring now used by many car dealers in order to determine whether or not their customers will be able to make their payments in full and on time, more individuals can afford a car in these dealerships. This is good news for car dealers as they can now offer more cars at cheaper rates. As a result, there is a higher demand for the automobiles that are sold, causing the sector to expand.

Some of the ways credit scoring has helped to increase the automobile industry is by helping to attract new buyers to purchase more cars and trucks at dealerships. Today, many people are able to purchase their first car from a dealership since they do not need perfect credit scores to qualify for loans. Many of these buyers have not taken care of their payments on time in the past and are able to take advantage of dealerships offering them new cars at a lower, possibly even zero down payment, interest rate. As a result, the demand for new automobiles has increased. Though this is good news for buyers, it also has bad side effects as more people can purchase cars but there are also more cars on the road. Research shows that most people have a negative perception of driving in a large city vehicle and many choose to buy small, fewer models' vehicles rather than larger ones. But nowadays many individuals are able to purchase even smaller vehicles due to all the pickups they can afford from large companies like Ford and Toyota. This may seem like good news, except for when there are accidents involving these vehicles. Lower to reasonable models of vehicles will cause more accidents because these cars do not have the protective features that the larger cars do. This is why car dealerships should offer financing for customers with poor credit scores, but they should also be careful and make sure there is enough incentive offered by the automobile industry to prevent this from happening.

It is important today for car dealerships to offer customers with little to no credit history, but this presents a problem because what if they cannot pay their payments in full and on time? In order to combat this problem, many dealerships feel as though they must increase interest rates to avoid default rates. This is a negative side effect of communication and credit scoring because people who do not have good or perfect credit scores will not be able to get a car loan but will still find the price of a car to be very expensive. Due to these higher interest rates, the automobile industry is susceptible to financial loss and this can negatively affect workers in their sales offices because many customers hold onto their payments due to the higher interest rates.

Though it may appear that selling more automobiles to people with bad credit is a terrific way for automakers to generate more money, there are some negative implications that could affect society as a whole if everyone's rates are hiked. If more individuals are raising their rates due to credit scoring, then families who do not have good or perfect credit will be without a vehicle. Though this is a problem, it could also bring about an increase in the trucking industry so as to provide more people with trucks to travel in. As long as there are enough incentives offered for companies to build cars for everyone and continue to make cars at a cheap price, then the automobile industry will be fine and continue to grow. However, if more individuals purchase fewer cars and trucks, there is less fuel available on the market which could cause another effect on society as a whole: the price of oil would rise and then other fuels may require higher prices. This would make it more difficult for families to travel and find jobs in other states or cities due to the higher prices of fuel.

Although many people approve of the idea of credit scoring, some people do not because of the fact that it can "lead to discrimination in lending access" and "impose limits on consumers' credit access and the amount they can borrow and pay back" (Finnigan, et al). This is true because of the fact that people are given a rough estimation of their creditworthiness, and this can limit their access to mortgages, credit cards, and other kinds of loans. However, this is only if they do not receive help from one of the several agencies who can provide assistance for them to get through the process. This issue could be solved by offering affordable loans that will help individuals with bad credit histories earn money in order to afford living expenses and eventually start paying back their debts.

Another problem associated with the existence of credit scoring is that it "is considered a form of consumer profiling" (Finnigan, et al). Consumer profiling is an invasion of consumers' privacy and can lead to the "creation of discriminatory markets" (Finnigan, et al). For example, a credit score might only be available to people whose net worth is above a certain number.

This could lead to loan prejudice. However, this problem could also be solved by offering affordable loans that will help individuals with bad credit histories earn money in order to afford living expenses and eventually start paying back their debts. Many creditors are not willing to offer this and would rather simply discriminate.

Advantages of Credit Scoring vs Traditional Approval

Vehicle buyers who have a good credit score will most likely be approved for their loan. In comparison to those with poor credit, those with good credit are more likely to buy vehicles and also less likely to default on their payments as well as pay the lender back in time. With traditional approval, the lender typically checks the applicant's employment history, background (i.e., criminal record), and asset/liability ratios.

If the applicant is found to have a clean background and good employment history, the lender may approve the loan which can be very risky because if the borrower defaults on their payments, it is very difficult to collect on these payments. Employers usually do not keep a record of their employees' credit histories which makes it hard for lenders to know whether or not they can trust the applicant with a loan. A lender's job is to assess risk when approving loans, however, if there is no information readily available, then there will be no way for them to do so accurately (or at least as accurately as possible). Credit scoring has been suggested as a solution for this problem.

Credit Scoring and the Automobile Industry

"The rapid expansion in credit scoring as a problem-solving tool in the recent two decades has been impacted by changes in loan legislation, accounting standards, and technology," according to the Federal Reserve Bank of St. Louis. These forces have resulted primarily from an increased focus on the ability of borrowers to repay loans and reduce risks."

Automobile lenders are concerned with their ability to accurately assess risk. It is very risky for them to approve loans for those that do not have good credit because if the borrower defaults on payments or cannot afford their payments, it will be very difficult for them to collect on these payments. It is a lot easier for the lender to determine if you have good or bad credit depending on your score.

The Auto Finance Sector and Credit Scoring are meant to benefit the consumer. It allows them to assess risk in a more efficient way than before. However, some have argued that this method is not appropriate for assessing risk because it does not take other factors into account such as job stability and employment history which are still important in determining whether or not you can afford your loan payments and whether or not you will be able to pay back the amount that you owe.

Chapter 8. Properly Dispute Negative Account

Negative subtleties on your credit report are terrible glaring tokens of your past monetary slip-ups. Or on the other hand, at times, the misstep isn't yours; however, a business or credit agency is to be faulted for credit report mistakes. In any case, it's dependent upon you to work to have negative credit report sections expelled from your credit report.

Evacuating negative data will assist you with accomplishing a superior credit score. A superior credit report is likewise the way to getting endorsed for credit cards and advances and to getting great loan fees on the records that you're affirmed for. To help with your approach to all the more likely credit, here are a few procedures to get negative credit report data expelled from your credit report.

Present a Dispute to the Credit Bureau

Credit report debates are most effortless when made on the web or through the mail. To make a debate on the web, you should have, as of late, arranged a duplicate of your credit report. You can present a question to the credit department who gave the credit report.

To debate by means of mail, compose a letter portraying the credit report and submit duplicates of any confirmation you have. The credit department examines your contest with the business that gave the data and expels the passage if they find that is, in reality, a blunder.

Contest with the Business That Reported to the Credit Bureau

Presently, you can totally sidestep the credit department and debate straightforwardly with the business that revealed the mistake to the credit authority, e.g., the credit card guarantor, bank, or obligation gatherer. You can make the contest recorded as a hard copy, and the business is required to do an examination simply like the credit bureau.

When the business establishes that there's to be sure a blunder on your credit report, they should notify all the credit departments of that mistake so your credit reports can be adjusted.

Send a Pay for Delete Offer to Your Creditor

You need to move toward precisely detailed negative data differently. Credit agencies won't expel exact, verifiable data regardless of whether you question it (because the examination will verify the exactness of this data), so you may need to haggle to have a few things expelled from your credit report.

Pay-for-erase offer is a method you can use with the reprobate or past due accounts. In a pay-for-erase arrangement, you offer to cover the record in return for having the negative subtleties expelled from your credit report. A few creditors will take you up on the offer.

Make a Goodwill Request for Deletion

With pay-for-erase, you can utilize cash as the negotiating concession for getting negative data expelled from your credit report. If you've just paid the record, be that as it may, you don't have much arranging power. Now, you can request kindness by mentioning a generosity deletion.

In a letter to the creditor, you may depict why you were late, state how you've since been a decent paying client, and ask that the records be accounted for much better. Once more, creditors don't need to consent and some won't. Then again, a few creditors will make these erasures if you converse with the correct individual.

Hold up Out the Credit Reporting Time Limit

If all else fizzles, your lone decision is to trust that those negative things will tumble off your credit report. Luckily, the law just permits the most negative data to be accounted for seven years. The special case is liquidation, which can be accounted for up to 10 years. The other uplifting news is that negative data influences your credit scoreless as it gets more established and as you supplant it with positive data. The holdup may not be as difficult as you might suspect. Buyers can demand their own credit report for nothing like clockwork from the three significant revealing organizations. In this way, no doubt, you should demand a report after the maturing time frame to affirm.

It is essential to note, in any case, that while the credit detailing organization will commonly erase the negative data from the report after the seven-year maturing period, data may, in any case, be kept on a document and can be discharged in specific situations. Those conditions incorporate when going after a position that pays over a specific sum, or applying for a credit line or a life protection strategy worth over a specific sum. Contingent upon where you live there might be progressively positive guidelines under state law, for example, a shorter legal time limit. You should contact your state's Attorney General's office for more data.

Meanwhile, you can improve your credit by making convenient installments on accounts you despite everything have open and dynamic.

What Doesn't Work

Petitioning for financial protection doesn't expel negative data from your credit report. If and when your obligations are released, the parities will be accounted as $0, however, the records will stay on your credit report. Also, accounts that were remembered for your insolvency will be noted all things considered.

Shutting a record won't kill the wrongdoing announcing. If you close a record with a past due to equalization, your installment will even now be accounted as reprobate until you get up to speed with the payment. The main thing shutting a record does is shield you from utilizing it.

Paying a reprobate parity doesn't delete the negative section on your credit report. When you pay the equalization, the record status will change to "current" or "all right" as long as the record isn't charged-off or in assortments. Charge-offs and assortment records will keep on being accounted for that path considerably after you pay the parity.

How to get rid of blunders on your report

Blunders on purchaser credit reports can be a typical event. That commits realizing how to debate an error on your credit report significant. If you discover something in your credit report that doesn't have a place there, this is what to do.

Stage 1 – Identify any credit report blunders

Audit your credit reports occasionally for wrong or deficient data. At annualcreditreport.com, you may acquire one free credit report from each of the three major credit bureaus—Equifax, Experian, and TransUnion—once a year. You can also purchase, usually at a cost, a credit checking service and analyze your report on a monthly basis.

Some basic credit report blunders you may spot include:

- Character errors, for example, an off-base name, telephone number, or address.
- A purported blended document that contains account data having a place with another customer. This may happen when you and another shopper have the equivalent or comparative names.
- A record erroneously credited to you because of data fraud.
- A shut record that is as yet being accounted for as open.
- An inaccurate detailing of you as a record proprietor, when you are only an approved client on a record.
- A record that is erroneously marked as late or reprobate, which could incorporate obsolete data, for example, a late installment that is more than 7 years of age or a mistaken date with respect to your last installment.
- A similar obligation was recorded more than once.
- A record registered more than once with different creditors.
- Wrong record adjusts.
- Mistaken credit limits.

How a Blunder on Your Credit Report Can Influence You

Is it extremely important to keep close tabs on your credit report? Can one mistake truly affect you? Indeed. Your credit report provides a wealth of information about you, such as how you manage your debts and if you've ever applied for financial assistance. You could be affected adversely by a mistake on your credit report from numerous points of view.

To begin, comprehend that credit revealing organizations sell the data in your credit reports to bunches that incorporate bosses, back up plans, service organizations, and numerous different gatherings that need to utilize that data to verify your character and assess your creditworthiness.

For example, if a service organization surveys your credit history and finds a not exactly ideal credit report, they may offer fewer good terms to you as a client. While this is called hazard-based evaluating and organizations must notify you if they're doing this, it can, in any case, affect you. Your credit report additionally may influence whether you can get an advance and the provisions of that advance, including your financing cost.

Stage 2 — Contact the furnisher

Your subsequent stage is to contact the furnisher or the organization that gave the wrong data, which could be an element like your bank or a service organization. Verify their records and affirm the mistake. You might have the option to determine the issue now. If the issue can't be settled, contact the credit detailing department straightforwardly.

Stage 3 – Credit Report's Errors

Under the Fair Credit Reporting Act, both the credit announcing agency and the organization that reports the data about you to the credit department are required to acknowledge questions from buyers—and right any wrong or inadequate data about you in that report.

The U.S. Government Trade Commission (FTC) suggests taking these activities:

- Tell the credit authority, recorded as a hard copy, what data you believe is mistaken. The Federal Trade Commission gives an example contest letter that makes this progression simpler. The letter traces what data to incorporate, from introducing the realities to mentioning that the blunder be expelled or remedied.

- Incorporate duplicates, not firsts, of materials that help your position.
- Consider encasing a duplicate of your credit report with the mistakes circumnavigated or featured.
- Send your letter by certified mail with "return receipt mentioned"—to guarantee the letter is conveyed. Keep your mail station receipt.
- Keep duplicates of all that you send.

Where to Send Your Contest Letter

Send your credit report contest letter to the credit announcing authority, just as to the organization that revealed the wrong data about you.

Stage 4 – Allow time for the examination

Credit revealing agencies must examine the contested things. The procedure, as a rule, takes less than 30 days. They're required to send important data to the data supplier—which means, whoever detailed the contested thing. The supplier must research the debate and report back to the credit announcing department.

If you're correct—and it is a blunder—the data supplier needs to notify the three significant credit authorities so they can address the data in your credit reports.

A Pointless Credit Report Contest

The credit agency or the organization that gave the data (the furnisher) likewise can verify that your case is negligible, in which matter they can choose not to research your case. In any case, they hould tell you they've declined to examine your question by composing a notification within five days.

Chapter 9.   The Truth About Credit Bureaus

Credit Bureaus are among the few organizations that can help you shape what happens in your financial world. Their presence, accuracy, errors, and general policies can affect your chances of getting financial support affect any person or firm in the world today. Without mincing words, it is okay not to understand religious organizations, social organizations, or certain niches in the business world. But Credit bureaus? Nobody gets far in the business world without them. It is even wrong to start taking up loans and credits without having vital information on companies like these, and that's why I will tell you about them now. You will learn how vital they are to your credit too.

For a start, what exactly is a credit bureau? A credit bureau is a well-established organization that is saddled with the job of keeping and supplying related information on your credit every time you need it. They are usually called Credit Reporting Agencies because that's the top of what they do; report your credit. Credit bureaus or credit reporting agencies are usually specialized companies or organizations that take up the job of collecting, compiling, and providing every necessary information on your credit when you need it. This is usually packed up and reported in the document formally known as 'credit report'.

Now, what is a credit report? It's a well-researched compilation of facts about your credit. The research is all done by your credit bureau; they only provide the details when you need them. They provide all related information that may help you decide how well you have handled your credit information. That would include some statistics such as your personal information, your credit information (the firms you have drawn credits with and what types of credit you have drawn), the previous judgments you have had based on finance, and your current credit score. You already have a good idea of what comprises your credit score.

Your credit reporting agencies are expected to provide you a free credit report once a year, and they may produce more than one on a charged basis. You may write to them to provide your credit information to certain companies. Usually, credit companies with which you are in a transaction already or from which you are about obtaining some credit. Credit Bureaus may provide your credit information when ordered by a court or the government, and definitely, your insurance company naturally gets a copy apart from cases where overviews of credit information are used in researches.

Your Credit Bureau would usually begin operation the instant you create a profile with them, and you instruct your credit companies to forward details of your credit transactions to them. For instance, you create a credit profile with TransUnion, a notable credit reporting agency in the United States. Then, you instruct your credit card companies to forward reports of your transaction with them to TransUnion, your credit Bureau. This means you expect your credit card company to supply reports on the type of loan you have drawn with them, how well you can pay up, and their overall impression of your payment style. Such information would be supplied with your full name, the time you drew the loans, the time you are expected to pay it all, and clauses you have added during the deal. They are not expected to speak in your favor or against you, but only supply the information they gather about your interaction to the credit bureau.

It is the same thing when you take secured loans, you surely remember credit cards offer unsecured loans. If you draw up a student loan, mortgage, or any other type of debt you may refer to as good or bad debt, you are drawing a secured loan. You may instruct your lenders to forward details of your transaction with them too. It is not necessary, but it is always advised since the next lender will likely lend you based on how impressed they are when they read and verify your previous debts, particularly how well you handled your last debt. The whole idea of credit scores and credit reporting centers on that.

Credit Bureaus do not collect all of your information, but are particular about only the pieces that relate to your credit, which will include statistics like "from whom did you draw credits, what were the policies agreed upon, what were the terms and how did you stick by them?" Your credit Bureaus then compile all of these bits and grade you on your performance in each and all of them. Some formats are followed when grading a credit report, and we will talk about every one of them in due time.

But we might begin by revealing more about the credit bureaus themselves. According to National Finance, there are three major credit reporting agencies in the US, they are TransUnion, Experian, and Equifax. American Bankers also report that these three are backed by different credit Acts in the US and they may request your credit records, your financial history, and certain personal information that may help them trace and compact your performance in credit dealings, even without informing you. Let's read up a bit on them:

1. TransUnion: If you'd like to judge them by the number of people they cover, TransUnion is the smallest of the three credit bureaus that are recognized in the United States, but it holds the widest range. It covers no less than 30 different countries in the world, including the United Kingdom. It provides demographic data and analytics alongside credit reports, and it is considered among the most reliable of the credit bureaus in the world. By 2020, TransUnion would be 52 years since establishment.
2. Experian: Experian was established only 23 years ago (as of 2019), so it is usually considered the youngest of the three by age. But nonetheless, Experian stands among the most reliable credit reporting agencies in the country. It is most popular in countries across Europe and of course the United States, and it has headquarters in world countries. It renders the same services as TransUnion, and it records information on more than 200 million citizens in the US alone.
3. Equifax: The oldest largest and most popular in the United States, Equifax is the third of the main credit companies recognized in the US. It keeps the record of well over 800 million people, besides millions of business profiles. Equifax holds an impressive record of credit keeping across all states in the US, and as such, it is often recognized as others.

According to American Bankers, the three organizations are charged with three major assignments — collecting your information, making an analysis of what they got, and making that available to due companies, and certainly, yourself. Every other credit bureau is charged with the same assignment, but it is worthy of note that about 100 other credit bureaus exist, only that they are rarely accessible to all citizens.

Each of these credit bureaus is expected to provide a free credit report to each individual on request. They must also present an avenue through which citizens may refute and challenge the statistics in their credit report. This means that if you receive your credit report and you observe some statistics that have doubts about, you may reach your credit bureau and have the error corrected.

How does your credit reporting agency get reports on your credit?

Credit bureaus require information, and they need to find it in some way. It is the only way they can have enough records to provide when you request your credit information, and they are protected by the Fair Credit Reporting Act in the US. This Act grants them the license to collect information on everyone they can and compile this information with the SS Number of each person. It is interesting to note that each agency has its method of getting information. This is why certain information may reflect in the report of a company and may be missing in the report of others.

Generally, what exactly do they need about you and how should they get your information?

The information credit bureaus usually require include:

1. Your data: The immediate data with which you want to be recognized is important. Your full name, your financial history, your social security number, and so forth. It has to match with what you have got on other papers. Credit bureaus try to see to it that your information is genuinely yours, and information belonging to someone with a similar name is not mixed up. It is worthy of note that credit companies or credit

bureaus do not require your bank account details, your income scale, or such statistics. They are only interested in what directly accounts for your credit.

2. Your credit information: This is other important information the credit bureau set out to collect. Your credit bureau gathers your credit history, your past and present credit deals, and your commitment to each of them, as well as the rate at which your credit information can influence your credit score. It actually determines how high or low your credit score is, alongside a few other features.

3. Public Judgment: Public judgment can be an eye-opener for lending companies. If you have been vindicated in many court cases, it may prove to lenders that you are a brilliant debtor who must be venerated. It may also be the reason your lenders are skeptical if they realize you have poor public judgments, you have defaulted on many loans and you had to result to a range of alternatives before them.

4. Recent Inquiries: Lastly, the total number of firms that have recently inquired about your credit report is included in the credit report. The names and profiles of the firms, the form of deal you propose to them, and so on are bits of information that your credit reporting agency may also set out to find.

So, how do they find all this data?

1. From your creditors: The most certain source of information is your creditors. They have records of how you performed in your debts. They usually submit a regular update on all of their clients to the credit bureaus, except in cases when the debtor requests that their credit information should not be sent to a credit bureau. In other cases, you may have to notify your credit company to supply your credit bureau with your credit information. Besides, public judgments and your recent inquiries, your credit companies usually supply the main information your firm is simple. Usually, your creditors are Credit Unions or banks.

2. The court: The court is another reliable source of information. The court provides a variety of information, ranging from public judgments to records of foreclosure,

bankruptcy, and similar situations. The court naturally provides this information to the public record, and also sends them to credit bureaus the instant they are updated.

Chapter 10. How Your Credit Repair Score Is Calculated

The credit score is calculated using several pieces of your credit report. If you want to have a high credit score or have good credit, you must know how it is calculated and what factors (banks and credit agencies) must approve or deny a loan or credit card.

Your credit score is calculated based on these categories, namely:

- The amounts that you owe
- The history of Payment
- What types of open accounts you have
- The age of the accounts
- The number of credit applications

Let's examine these factors and see how we can raise your credit score one by one.

The Amounts That You Owe

It is no coincidence that the amounts you owe are the next thing to discuss. This is because, after the history of payment, it is known to be the next most influencing factor of your credit score.

It is already a general rule that you are required to use only 30% of the credit the bank approves and nothing more than that. It will be highly unwise if you use all the credit that the bank approves, say $300 on a $1000 credit card. That means you should never make use of the maximum account allowed on your card.

Credit bureaus perceive this as an omen when you start to depend on the money, and they tend to withdraw as it signifies a negative mark for your credit report and your credit score.

I would advise you to use below 30% of your credit, or what's best is you could go ahead to use only 10% of your credit line and nothing more than that. By doing this, you will have better credit scores, and your chances of increasing and even sustaining a good credit score will be limitless.

The amount of money you owe is also a key factor to consider when calculating your score.

The History of Payment

Consider making payments on or even earlier than the agreed time, as it is absolutely important and has a major impact on your score. If you make late payments, then your credit score will dramatically reduce.

The fundamental thing a lender would want to find out is whether or not you paid your bills or even your credit loans in good time. This category, out of the others, majorly influences your credit score and makes up to 35% of your score, which is why it is very important to take note of it.

Now that you know that delayed payments can affect your credit score and hinder you from building a good credit history, you must ensure you pay all debts on time without any qualms.

The types of accounts normally considered for payment history are namely:

- Installment Loans
- Credit Cards (such as Visa, Master Card, and so on)
- Loans to the consumer
- Retail accounts and;
- Mortgage Loans

Remember, making and building a good credit score is a path that will require you to make payments on time.

What Types of Open Accounts You Have?

Another factor that can favor your credit score is having various types of loans (mortgages, cars, and student loans) and credit cards.

Your credit score is majorly concerned with the different types of credit you use, some of which exist are credit cards, mortgage loans, installment loans, and accounts with finance companies.

Note that it is not so important that you use each one of them, and I'll advise that you only open accounts that you are going to use.

The credit mix has no major effect on your credit score, but it is of great importance that your credit report does not contain excess information on which your score is based.

There is no perfect version of a credit mix as it varies with time from individual to individual. Opening car loans, student loans, and credit cards you won't be needing won't be advisable for you.

It would be an added advantage to have this factor that shows that you know how to handle your credit responsibly.

The Age of the Accounts

Consistency is key in the credit score world. As long as you keep maintaining a good credit score history, your credit score will always remain high. The general rule of thumb explains this because the longer you have credit cards, the more your credit score will increase. That's why I'll advise you to start your credit as soon as you can. This is a factor that constitutes about 15% of your credit score, measuring the length at which you have your credit accounts and how well you have managed them within that period.

Here is what your FICO credit score records:

- It considers the age of both the new and old accounts and even the average age of all of your accounts.
- It also considers your credit lines (if you have), how long you have been with them and how your payment history has been.

- Finally, it measures your loans/credit cards' exact age. Because of this, many professionals advise that older accounts should neither be closed nor canceled, as it is likely to affect your credit score.

There's a high possibility of you having a high credit score by having a long time with your credit.

The Number of Credit Applications

Lastly, the number of applications to your credit slightly affects your credit score. Every time you apply for a loan or possibly a credit card (even if not yet approved), your credit score slightly decreases.

Opening various credit accounts within a very short time can be very risky for financial institutions, especially when it's a case of one who does not have a lengthy credit history. This explains why many people see that their credit score has decreased either when they open a credit card or when they are approved for a particular loan. However, the decline is temporary.

Also, bear in mind that credit checks vary. Interestingly, checking your credit will have your credit score reduced if and only if it is a hard inquiry. There are hard inquiries and soft inquiries, which I will explain below.

A hard inquiry is made when a loan is applied to a lender. That may include a student loan, car, mortgage loan. These inquiries affect your credit score.

While the soft inquiry is made when you request a copy of your credit report, apply for a job, or use it for a credit monitoring service. These types of inquiries in no way affect your credit score.

How Exactly Is It Calculated?

As important as it is to calculate your credit score, it is also very important to know that these factors have no fixed percentage. They may vary due to the financial information obtained from your credit report.

This goes to say that without adequate knowledge of the basic factors above, there is a tendency for an individual to be careless in the decisions he makes at obtaining a high credit score. It is hence very important that these factors are known.

Though these factors are applied when calculating a credit report, the level of importance varies from person to person.

It is not possible to record the impact of each factor on the credit score without acknowledging the report as a whole.

How to Check Your Credit Score

Some services enable you to check your credit score at very little or no cost. However, you must take caution and use services that you know are reliable so that you don't fall into the hands of scammers on the Internet. Some of these reliable services, especially those listed below, have no cost.

Chapter 11.   The Fico Credit Scores

Fair Isaac Corporation—the business that produces "FICO" ratings—is the oldest and most omnipresent credit scoring agency. Fair Isaac claims over 80% of investors use their ratings. Factors considered by Fair Isaac as credit scores come up include:

- Payment history (about 35% of the score): the company is looking at things like whether you have paid on time, have any overdue payments, declared bankruptcy, how current past due accounts are, or if you have rulings against you. This is the bulk of your score, so it's the most important. Late payments, settlement claims, settled accounts, repossessions, foreclosures, and public record issues such as tax liens, convictions, or bankruptcies can have a significant negative impact on your FICO score, according to Fair Isaac. Even getting a payment just one month late can have a negative impact on your ranking.
- Amounts owed on credit accounts (about 30% of the score): FICO looks at things like the amounts that you be obliged, and how many of your accounts hold a balance. The principal way to improve this part of your score is to pay down your outstanding debt. Your credit history has a period of around 15% of the score. Longer credit history usually yields a higher ranking.
- New credit (about 10% of the score): Fair Isaac wants to see a credit history built rather than a lot of new accounts. Opening up multiple accounts in a short time may mean a higher risk. Depending on the reason, hard inquiries about your account may also lower your score. For example, if your credit report is reviewed by a variety of borrowers, it might seem like you are actively applying for new credit. That is why, when shopping for new credit, it is important to be careful. Above all, used car dealers always want to get you to sign a form that requires them to peek at your credit report, even if you're just shopping in the store. Don't consider that until you are adamant about entering into an agreement. But as long as you're doing all of your car or home mortgage comparison shopping within about 30 days or so, it shouldn't have a lot of

effect on your ranking. Don't think about inquiries too much, they make up just a small fraction of your FICO score. According to FICO, the number of requests is typically not a major factor in your credit score— an investigation will probably lower your score by less than 5 points, even if outside a small shopping window for reference. So, FICO states that once the investigation is longer than 12 months it does not include inquiries in its ratings.

- Types of credit (about 10% of the score): Fair Isaac is offering a "healthy mix" of different credit forms, including revolving loans (such as credit cards) and maintenance plans (such as a mortgage or car loan). You can see that about 65% of your FICO score depends on whether you pay your bills on time (35%) and whether the balance you owe is too high for your credit limits (30%). You may have more than one FICO score as Fair Isaac now provides a number of FICO rating models that highlight different aspects of your performance, and because a FICO score is dependent on your credit report, and each of the three national credit reporting agencies may have very different information on you, the ratings may vary from each of the three organizations.

What Is a Good FICO Score?

FICO scores range between 300 and 850. Fair Isaac reports that just fewer than 40% of Americans have more than 750 FICO ratings, which most borrowers would find very strong. Equifax claims most FICO scores usually fall between the 600s and 700s and offers these estimates:

- 20% are above 780.
- 20% are in the range of 745–780.
- 20% are in the range of 690–745.
- 20% are in the range of 620–690.
- 20% are below 619.

Fair Isaac offers a free calculator that you can use to see how different credit ratings can influence how much you're getting credit for. Go to www.myfico.com and click "Education," then "Credit basics," then scroll down on the left and click "Improve your score," then click on "See how much money you can save" in the article.

Most Common Reasons for Negative Credit Decisions

Underneath are the most common reasons for negative credit decisions, according to Equifax. You can see how these fit in with the way you score credit files.

- Serious offense.
- Extreme delinquency and a filed or triggered public record.
- It is too new or uncertain since the offense.
- The level of account criminality is too high.
- The percentage of delinquency accounts is too high.
- Money owed too high on deposits.
- The percentage of credit-limit balances to revolving accounts is too high.
- The length of time the account is set is too short.
- Too many balance accounts.

The FICO Scoring Model

FICO has the reputation of being the most trustworthy scoring model, given its extensive track record. The Fair Isaac Company started calculating these values in 1989. They've updated the algorithms several times over the last three decades to account for changing factors and ensure that they continue to yield consistent credit ratings.

The standard FICO score approach will give you a score between 300 and 850. A score of less than 600 is considered low. It is considered exceptional if your score is greater than 740. Between 600 to 740, creditworthiness varies from medium to above-average.

FICO debuted its FICO 9 scoring model in 2014. The main change in this model was to downplay the significance of unpaid medical expenses. The explanation for this is that unpaid medical debts are not true financial health indicators. You could be waiting for insurance to pay a medical payment, or you could be completely uninformed that medical debt has been sent to a collection agency. For some people, this important change allowed their credit score to increase by up to 25 points.

Other amendments made in 2017 made it illegal for collectors to report late medical bills that were not yet 180 days past due. The three credit reporting bureaus also removed all data on civil judgments and tax lien records from their systems in 2017. According to FICO, this improved the scores of about 6% of individuals.

FICO 8 (which the company developed in 2009) was the standard credit-score version before FICO 9. The FICO 8 score is still the most widely used in the lending business. The differentiating elements of FICO 8 were that it penalized you for charging near your total credit limit each month and granted you forgiveness if you had only one 30-day late payment.

It's worth mentioning that when FICO updates its scoring algorithms, lenders have the option of keeping their current version or upgrading. Because upgrading to the new model is so expensive, FICO 8 has remained the clear preference. Even FICO 5 models are still used by some lenders. During the application process, you can inquire about the model your lender is employing.

In most cases, FICO ratings do not alter significantly in the short term. If you start missing payments or showing charge-offs and defaults, this is an exception. FICO scores aren't available to everyone. If you don't have credit, you'll be classified as "credit invisible," according to experts.

To get a FICO score, you must have six months of payments recorded to the credit bureaus.

What Is a FICO Score?

The credit score structure was formulated by the Fair Isaac Corporation also referred to as FICO. This credit score is utilized by financial institutions. There are other credit score models; however, the FICO score is the one that is most commonly used. Consumers can get and keep high credit scores by simply making sure their debt level remains low, and they maintain an extended history of paying their bills as and when they are due.

In the FICO scoring formula, not all credit reports are scored equally. Credit scores are weighted based on the particular "scorecard" that a person falls under. For example, if the person has filed for bankruptcy, they may be scored using a special "bankruptcy" scorecard. The credit score for a person under one scorecard may be affected differently by a negative event, like a late payment, than of someone with the same event on a different scorecard.

The scorecard you're on is determined by the most recent significant event in your credit history. The first 10 scorecards go something like this:

Scorecards 1–5:

1. Those with public records, including judgments and bankruptcy, on their credit report.
2. For those with serious delinquencies other than bankruptcies (60, 90, 120 latest, collections, judgments, charge-offs repossessions, etc.).
3. Those with only 1 credit account (very thin files).
4. Those with only 2 credit accounts (thin files).
5. Those with 3 credit accounts only.

Scorecards 6–10 should not have any grave felonies (the definition of "serious" is unknown).

6. 0–2 year's oldest account.
7. 2–5 year's oldest account.
8. 5–12 year's oldest account.
9. 12–19 year's oldest account.
10. 19+ years oldest account.

There is a total of 12 scorecards, and they are subject to change as FICO (formerly Fair Isaac Corp) updates its scoring formula.

Chapter 12. Simple Steps to Fix Your Credit Scores

Improving your credit score can mean qualifying for lower financing costs and better terms. That is genuine whether you need a decent credit score to acquire cash for individual reasons (a home advance, a vehicle advance, to get a credit card, and so forth) or so you can buy stock, rent an office, and so on, to begin or develop your business.

The issue is, credit fix is similar to improving your expert system: You possibly consider it when it is important. However, if you don't have great credit, it's almost difficult to address that circumstance short-term.

That is the reason an opportunity to begin fixing your credit is currently - before you truly need it.

Luckily, it's not too difficult to improve your credit score.

Here's a basic procedure you can follow:

1. Audit your credit reports.

The credit authorities - TransUnion, Equifax, and Experian - are required to give you a free duplicate of your report once every year. You should simply inquire. (Snap the connections to demand a duplicate.)

Another approach to see your credit reports is to utilize free assistance like Credit Karma. (I'm not supporting Credit Karma. I like it and believe it's convenient. However, I'm certain other free administrations are similarly as valuable.)

When you've joined, you can see your credit scores and view the data contained on the reports. As a rule, the passages on the different reports will be the equivalent, however not generally. For an assortment of reasons, credit reports are infrequently indistinguishable.

2. Debate negative imprints.

In the past times, you needed to compose letters to the credit departments if you needed to question blunders. Presently benefits like Credit Karma (once more, I'm not supporting CK and just reference it because I've utilized it) let you contest blunders on the web.

Simply ensure you get the most blast for your debate endeavors. Certain variables gauge more vigorously on your credit score than others, so focus on those things first.

Start with critical imprints like assortment records and decisions. It's normal to have at any rate one assortment account show up on your report. I had two from medicinal services suppliers I utilized subsequent to having a cardiovascular failure; my insurance agency continued asserting it had paid while the suppliers said it had not, and in the long run the records wound up with an assortment organization. In the long run, I chose to pay the suppliers and contend with the insurance agency later. However, the two assortments ended up on my credit report.

Fixing those issues was simple. I tapped the "Contest" button, chose "The creditor consented to evacuate my obligation on this record," and inside seven days the debate was settled and the passage was expelled from my credit report.

You can likewise contest mistakes through each credit department. If that is your inclination, go here for TransUnion, here for Equifax, and here for Experian.

Remember a few questions will take longer than others. In any case, that is OK. When you start a contest, you're done: The credit departments are required to research it and report the goals.

Invest as much energy as it takes attempting to have deprecatory imprints expelled because they additionally weigh intensely on your general score.

3. Contest inaccurate late-installment sections.

Errors occur. Your home loan bank may report an installment was late that was in actuality paid on schedule. A credit card supplier may neglect to enter an installment accurately.

You can contest late installments - regardless of whether in accounts that are present or records that have been shut - a similar way you debate deprecatory imprints.

Your installment history is another factor that weighs vigorously on your credit score, so make a solid effort to tidy up those mistakes.

4. Choose if you need to play the game some credit fix organizations play.

So far, we've talked about attempting to expel off base data as it were. You can, if you pick, likewise debate exact data.

For instance, say a record went to assortment, you never paid it, and the assortment organization surrendered. All that remaining parts are the passage on your credit report. You can even now decide to debate the section. Numerous individuals do. What's more, in some cases those sections will get evacuated.

Why? When you enter a question the credit authority requests that the creditor verify the data. Some will. Many, similar to assortment offices, won't. They'll basically overlook the solicitation - and if they do disregard the solicitation, the office is required to expel the passage from your credit report.

This means littler firms, similar to assortment organizations or nearby loan specialists or little to average size specialist organizations, are less inclined to react to the credit departments. It's an issue they needn't bother with. Banks, credit card organizations, automobile fund organizations, and home loan moneylenders are much bound to react.

So, if you need - and I'm not suggesting this, I'm trying to say it's a system a few people choose to utilize - you can contest data in the expectation the creditor won't react. (This is the methodology many credit fix firms use to attempt to improve their customers' scores.) If the creditor doesn't react, the passage gets expelled.

5. Ask pleasantly.

Possibly you attempted and neglected to evacuate a negative remark, a late installment, or a record that was checked "Paid as concurred" (which may mean the creditor consented to let you pay short of what you owed). Would it be advisable for you to surrender? Not a chance. Take a stab at asking pleasantly.

Creditors can educate credit agencies to expel sections from your credit report whenever. For instance, I hadn't charged anything on a specific credit card for quite a long time and didn't see that I had been charged my yearly expense until the installment was late. (Like a good for nothing, I was simply hurling the announcements without opening them because I "knew" there were no charges.)

The late installment appeared on my credit report, so I called the credit card organization, clarified what had occurred, that I had been a client for quite a long time, and inquired as to whether they would expel the section. They said sure. Furthermore, they additionally consented to forgo every single yearly charge later on. (Demonstrating once more that if you don't ask, you don't get.)

When all else comes up short, call and ask pleasantly. You'll be amazed by how often a courteous solicitation for help pays off.

6. Increment credit limits.

Another factor that weighs intensely on your credit score is your credit card usage: The proportion of accessible credit to credit utilized has a major effect. As a rule, conveying a parity of in excess of 50 percent of your accessible credit will contrarily affect your score. Maximizing your cards will hurt your score.

One approach to improve your proportion is to square away your equalizations. However, another route is to expand your credit limit. If you owe $2,500 on a card with a $5,000 cutoff and you get the limit expanded to $7,500, your proportion immediately improves.

To get credit limits expanded, call and ask pleasantly. If you have a nice installment history, most credit card organizations will gladly build your breaking point - all things considered, they need you to convey a high parity. That is the manner by which they bring in cash.

Simply ensure you don't really utilize the extra accessible credit, because then you'll be back in the equivalent accessible credit proportion pontoon... also, you'll be more profound paying off debtors.

7. Open another credit card account.

Another approach to expand your credit card usage proportion is to open another record. For whatever length of time that you don't convey an equalization on that card, your accessible credit quickly increments by that card's breaking point.

Attempt to get a card that doesn't charge a yearly expense, however. Your most solid option is through a bank where you as of now have a record. Without a doubt, cards with no yearly expense will in general charge higher loan fees. However, if you never convey an equalization, the financing cost is unessential.

Be that as it may, once more, be keen: The objective isn't to gain admittance to more money, the objective is to improve your credit score. If you think you'll be enticed to run up an equalization on another record, don't open one.

8. Pay down extraordinary adjusts.

I know. You need a higher credit score because you need to acquire cash; if you had the cash to square away your parities, then you won't have to obtain it.

As yet: diminishing your level of accessible credit utilized can make a brisk and significant effect on your credit score. So go on a no-frills financial plan to let loose money to settle your equalization. Or on the other hand, sell something.

Squaring away adjusts might be hard to pull off as a transient move to expand your credit score, yet it ought to be a piece of your drawn-out monetary arrangement. Not exclusively will your credit score increment after some time, you won't pay as much premium - which, if you consider it, is simply giving moneylenders cash you would prefer remained in your pocket.

9. Pay off high-intrigue, "new" credit accounts first.

Time of credit matters to your credit report. Financing costs matter to your ledger. If you have $100 every month to put toward squaring away adjusts (far beyond the necessary regularly scheduled installments, obviously), center around taking care of high intrigue accounts. Then organize those by the age of the record. Pay off the most up-to-date ones first; that way you'll build the normal length of credit, which should support your score, yet you'll additionally have the option to all the more rapidly abstain from paying moderately high intrigue.

Then put the cash not spent on that installment into the following record on your rundown. The "obligation snowball" framework truly accomplishes work.

10. Ride some extraordinary credit coattails (of an individual you trust.)

State your life partner has a credit card with practically zero parity and an incredible installment history; if the individual in question consents to include you as an approved client, from a credit score perspective you consequently advantage from her card's accessible credit just as her installment history.

Remember if the individual in question makes a late installment, that passage will show up as negative on your credit report as well.

So, pick your credit card companions carefully.

11. Keep your "old" credit cards.

Your period of credit history has a moderate yet at the same time important effect on your credit score. Let's assume you've had a specific credit card for a long time; shutting that record may diminish your general normal credit history and adversely sway your score, particularly over the present moment.

If you're planning to expand your credit score however you additionally need to dispose of a credit card account, dispose of your "most up to date" card.

12. Cover each tab on schedule.

Indeed, even one late installment can hurt your score. Do all that you can, from this day on, to consistently cover your tabs on schedule.

What's more, if one month you can't pay everything on schedule, be keen about which charges you pay late. Your home loan moneylender or credit card supplier will report a late installment to the credit departments, yet utilities and cell suppliers likely won't.

Check the "Records" segment on your credit reports to see which records are recorded and if you need to pay late, pick a record that doesn't show up on your report.

Then make a solid effort to ensure you can generally pay everything on time later on. Your credit score will thank you, thus will your feelings of anxiety.

What's more, after some time, so will your financial balance.

Chapter 13.   Is Credit Repair Ethical?

Many people struggle to pay their debts and have insufficient or poor credit scores. Credit repair would be an option for them if they knew how it worked or what the risks are. There are plenty of people who claim credit repair is unethical, but no studies have been made on whether or not this type of process is actually against the law."

Is Credit Repair Ethical?

The topic of "credit repair" has become more prevalent in society over recent years, as a lot more people struggle with debt and lack of credit. Dave Askin claims that credit repair is unethical, and books such as The Credit Repair Manual claim that it is against the law too.

Is credit Repair Legal?

The problem with credit repair is that many people don't trust parts of it as they believe they are using parts of credit repair services for illegal purposes. It's important to understand what is legal and what isn't, in order to be able to make informed decisions about your personal finances. Whether or not a particular company claims to offer an "ethical" process (whatever that means) or not really doesn't matter. You must be aware of the fact that nothing can absolutely be 100% ethical or legal in this world.

Credit Repair vs. Credit Rating

There are two different things that you need to understand /undefined [before] you can make a decision about how much credit repair is ethical for you. The first one is a credit rating. A credit rating is simply a numerical value that represents the probability of you being able to afford to pay back your debts in the future. It is an opinion of the likelihood that you will pay back your debts. Something you can check on freecreditreport.com and see for yourself what it says about your own personal situation by going to the page where they'll let you check out all three sections, and logging into your own account and doing it there.

The other thing is credit repair. In fact, it's the same thing as credit rating, it's just that the credit repair is not as accurate as a computerized scoring system. A computerized scoring system will be able to calculate your actual risk of default based on the data from all of your accounts held with different lenders and financial institutions and analyze that data in order to give you an accurate picture of whether or not you'll be able to pay back your debts in the future.

Dave Askin claims that credit repair is unethical. There is no proof to support the fact that credit repair companies do anything illegal, but it also cannot be proven that they do nothing illegal either. A lot of people claim that there are certain things credit repair companies will tell you to do or will fee you for doing and those things are against the law in some way.

The Prize Patrol Will Be Calling Soon...Yes, Really!

Many of the companies will charge you a fee for filling out a "credit dispute form" on your behalf with each of the three major consumer credit reporting agencies - Experian, Equifax, and TransUnion. Some of the companies will actually extend you money to engage in these activities, including charging your current account for the money they will get from Experian, Equifax, or TransUnion. Even if you don't fall for their line of bull and you call up and ask them to remove everything from your credit report that they charge you for (and they may just tell you "read the fine print") that is still a violation of federal law and should be reported.

Credit Repair Companies do take advantage of people. People who are desperate and will do whatever it takes to have their credit fixed. Companies that run these credit repair scams are exploiting people who don't know the laws about credit repair. The companies, many of them foreign, make millions of dollars, while the people they prey on get nothing for their money. Some companies will tell you that you can get your "credit report" for free and then charge you to "repair" your credit. This is what is technically called a "bait and switch." When they explain to you how much it will cost to fix your credit and you sign up and pay them money, they have made a false claim. If this is done with intent to defraud then it's against the law, regardless if they didn't attempt to hide it or anything like that.

Credit Repair Is Illegal

Whether or not credit repair is legal is a debatable subject. Dave Askin claims that credit repair is illegal, when, in fact, there has never been a single case in the United States Federal Court. This in itself is proof of the fact that credit repair and unsecured loans are completely separate things. Some companies claim they have an "official" relationship with the government and are authorized to handle disputes on your behalf. In reality, this means nothing because only a court can authorize something to be done legally, and you can't just go to any judge to get your debt removed from your report because it's a violation of Credit Card Laws which states "it shall be unlawful for any person...to ...make any false or fraudulent statement or representation."

You will also get ripped off if you take money from these companies. Some companies will charge you for a credit repair service that doesn't even exist. It is illegal to use or offer to use your identity for the purpose of committing a crime. If this is done, it is also called Identity Theft. This includes using your name and date of birth to prove that you are who you say you are in order to get money from someone else's account or more simply put, it is fraudulently using someone's identity in place of your own. Scammers do this all the time. Not only is it illegal it is a crime and can result in you being held responsible for any damages done to the person whose identity was misused.

Credit Repair Companies Are Not Licensed

You will see from the above quotes that credit repair is clearly not allowed. There are a lot of consumer protection laws in place to protect consumers, but the federal powers are limited. For example, credit repair companies are not regulated by the state of registration because they never asked for that license or were licensed there prior to moving to "TrueCredit."

According to the FTC, a person can't be licensed in two different states at the same time. However, since credit repair companies have no legitimate relationship with any governmental agency whatsoever the FTC does not have any power to stop them from operating. The Federal Trade Commission has been around for almost fifty years and has tried to protect consumers, but they don't have any authority over non-federal entities or companies. There isn't anything on paper that states the FTC can regulate credit repair characters, only state attorneys general can do so.

This is why every state has different laws about credit reporting and scores. Some states require the companies to be licensed, some do not. For example, Alabama requires all records to be kept for at least five years, but some states don't have any regulation in place whatsoever. Tennessee and Nevada are no regulations states and are free for anyone to operate in them. Consumers need to make sure they know what their state requirements are before they sign up with any of these companies.

Whenever you sign up with a credit repair company, they generally want your Social Security number or other personal information. This is very bad because you are giving them direct access to clean up your credit. But what is worse, these companies can do anything they like with your information and you can't stop them!

Children's Credit Is Protected by Law

If a minor under the age of eighteen requests a loan, no lender can approve it without the consent of their parent or guardian. Also, if a minor applies for credit on their own, any credit reporting agency is not allowed to include that information in their database if it affects the child's credit score.

There is also a federal law that prevents any adverse action against a minor for the first sixty days they are in possession of a credit card. This is designed to give the minor time to learn how to properly use their new credit card.

While there are many companies that will offer you to remove bad information from your credit report it's highly advised that before you do this, you need to know what they're about and more importantly, read their contract. What these companies do is offer a way for getting your report cleaned up but they ask clients for money in exchange for their services and often times the money isn't worth it.

However, if you have a loan with your credit card company and the information on your report is inaccurate, you can contact them to tell them about the problem. The only way to avoid repair fees for inaccurate information is if you notify them in writing of the problem within 90 days.

Q: I'm on my daughter's student account and we have had issues with it for months. If I cancel it now, will that help in getting rid of her debt?

A: It's not suggested that canceling this account will help get rid of any debt but it's safe to say that this will make things easier. Even if you do cancel this account, her name will still be on the account, but she won't be able to access it. You can also call the debt collector at XXXXXXXXXXXX and make payment arrangements for her. If she can't pay the bills then she will need to talk with these companies to dispute the accounts and stop making payments until they're removed.

Q: Tried using my credit card today and it was denied. The last time I used it I made a purchase for $600. What could this mean? How could this have happened?

A: It's impossible to tell what is going on without knowing more information about your situation. Are you paying off any debt that you have? Do you owe taxes? Does it hurt your credit score if your purchase was declined? Have you ever had this problem before with this card or any other card?

Q: My mother is 65 years old and still has student loans that she hasn't been able to pay off yet. I'm her daughter and want to help her but don't know what to do. Can I use my credit score to help her pay off this loan?

A: If your mother co-signed for these loans then she will be responsible for them even though they were given out before she was of the age of majority. You can't help her or get a personal loan for this. Even if you used your credit cards to pay off these debts you would still be responsible for them, but it may show up on your credit report.

Q: I received a notice that my student loans were up for review and also a notice that my bankruptcy was reviewed. How do I know which one it is?

A: This is something that would likely show up on your credit report unless there was an agreement between the two of you and it was removed. If there is a debt or creditors have issues with you, then these could be applications to review your debts so they can clear them from their records.

Chapter 14.   Why People and Companies Need Credit Repair

First of all, we'll talk about the two main reasons that you may need credit repair. You may need it for personal reasons, such as a medical or dental emergency, or to pay for something important like a home or car, or you may need it to get business transactions off the ground.

Once we've covered those two areas, we'll move on to how credit works and how it can be designed to work in people's favor. Finally, we'll finish with how you can go about getting access to a good credit repair service if you feel that you're too far gone for anything else.

Personal Credit Repairs

Let's start by looking at when people need credit repair for personal reasons. In these days of economic uncertainty, it's good to know that there are some ways to minimize the cost of living so that you don't have to choose between putting food on the table and paying bills. One way to do this is by using a service like ours as we update your credit score regularly and get rid of incorrect information.

You might have engaged in a real estate transaction recently and were asked to prove your financial viability before signing on the dotted line. If this was the case then you needed good credit scores or it wouldn't have been possible for you to proceed with the transaction at all.

Many companies today require good credit scores before they will deal with you. When you read reports about poor people being turned down for loans, it's not because they're bad people, but because they have high levels of debt. You could have a lot of debt and still be a good person with a benevolent nature. If you do have credit records that haven't been updated for a long time, there's no guarantee that other people will see through this even if you're doing well.

High levels of debt are a sign that money has been spent faster than it has been earned and this can lead to problems in the future if you spend more than you earn all the time. It's not liked a person needs to live like a pauper, but it does help to be careful about how much you spend and what you spend it on. When a person uses their credit card constantly to pay for everyday expenses, the problem of debt can spiral out of control.

People make mistakes all the time. You might have been using your credit card for a number of years but then missed one payment by mistake. This means that your credit score is now under threat as bad information has been added to your file. That will lead lenders to think twice about doing business with you in the future because they'll be reluctant to lend money.

The main issue with personal credit repair is that it's hard to tell how much you need to improve your score. After all, if you can't even pay off your debt then it seems like you'll always struggle. On the other hand, if you can repay everything on time and at a low level of interest then the interest will be lower than if you had chosen a more frivolous pastime that led to high levels of debt.

The best way in these circumstances is to look for a credit repair service. A good one will give you straight answers so that you know what needs to be done so that your score can improve. From there it's up to you to make the right choices and get going.

Business Credit Repairs

Most of us are aware of how credit works when we buy a new car or house. It's not like we have to learn from scratch, but it can be hard to pinpoint where the problems lie when things turn sour. It's like a person who has been walking and suddenly falls over. At first, they can't imagine what happened, but then they realize that their shoelaces came undone and tripped them up. This is what people need to know about business credit in order to get it right.

The first thing that businesses need is a high level of business credit repair for a variety of reasons. If you're planning on doing business with a particular organization, then they will want to know that you have suitable credits in place before they can proceed. It's not just for your own protection, but because it helps them out too. They'll be able to trust their money isn't going to go wrong and hand over the cash more easily if this goes ahead without fault or delay from your end.

Business credit repair is also important for people who are building new financial initiatives from scratch by opening up multiple accounts with different banks and loan providers. It's easy to put down your money and get the loan, but at the end of the day, you also have to keep everything up to date. Keeping a score on your finances is hard enough as it is, but when there are other people involved then it can be trickier still.

Some companies do their own credit referencing and this usually involves a third party who keeps on top of things in order to make sure that everyone is eligible for a loan or service. Having information from various banks on file will give clients more peace of mind when they choose their bank partners because they'll know if they're at high risk or not. It means that any potential problems are put out of the way before they become real issues for an organization or person.

Credit reporting companies are also in business to do background checks on potential customers or clients before they can go ahead and lend money. This is a big issue for both borrowers and lenders, as you'll now know exactly what type of person you're dealing with. A good credit repair service will have this information to hand so that you always know exactly what it is they plan to do with your information.

These things aren't impossible to fix if you want them fixed, which is why businesses rely on help. They don't want the problem with their records to become their downfall and turn into a source of difficulty later down the line. A good business credit repair service will do what it can to help you get back on track so that you can do well in the future.

Make the Phone Call

You've just had a great idea for a business and now you want to make it happen, only it's not that simple. You're going to need money and lots of it, but how are you going to convince people to trust you? Putting your money where your mouth is liked something that proves you're serious about what needs doing here. It shows other people you want what they have and the only way they'll get it is if they trust you enough with their cash long enough to see results.

That's why credit repair is so important for small businesses, because it can give them the edge that they need to get their ideas off the ground. It might be that you've got an idea for a new kind of product or service that everyone will want to try out. If this is true, then it's going to save you a lot of money in the long run. You won't have to put out cash right away which is always nice and let's be honest, everyone likes to save as much as they can from time to time.

You Can Do It with Credit Repair

Credit repair is the key to success when it comes to starting a new venture and there's no denying that. If you need proof of this, then you should just look at the small business credit repair services in your area. Many of these companies are going out of their way to help people get on track and start a new career or maybe even a lifestyle change. You want your plans to succeed so that you can be successful and with this sort of help, they just might. The best thing about credit repair is that it's so easy to get going on. You don't have to file anything with a credit agency and there's nothing you have to do other than keep an eye on how your credit score is going. You can do it without any hassle or any extra work and in the meantime, you can start making some serious money.

You Can Do It with High-Interest Rates

There are lots of ways that you can save money but only a few of them are easy for most people. You need to realize that there's a high level of competition out there for money so if you go down this road, then you're going to have to go up against some very tough competition. This means that your chances of succeeding in this game are simply not very good. Good for you!

Chapter 15. Effective Strategies for Repairing Your Credit

Pay-to-Delete Strategy

If you have derogatory items in your credit report, you can opt to pay the credit balance only if the creditor agrees to delete the items from your credit report. As I already mentioned, don't agree to a $0 balance appearing on your credit report since this taint your reputation. This will ultimately improve your rating. Actually, the idea is to ensure that, whatever amount you agree to pay, it doesn't show up as your last date of the activity. If the creditor only cares about their money, why should they bother telling the world that you have finally paid?

In most instances, the creditors often write off debts within just 2 years of constant defaulting, after which this information is sold in bulk to a collection company for some pennies of a dollar. This means that the collection companies will even be just fine if you even pay a fraction of what you ought to pay. Whatever you pay, they will still make money! This makes them open to negotiations such as pay-to-delete since they have nothing to lose, anyway.

- Therefore, only use the pay-to-delete approach at this level and not at any other. Actually, the only other way around it for the collection company is a judgment, which can be costly, so you have some advantage here.
- Additionally, use this strategy when new negative items start showing up on your report that could hurt your reputation as a credit consumer.
- Also, since the creditors will often sell the same information to multiple collection companies, you might probably start noting the same debt being reported by several companies; use pay-to-delete to get them off your report.
- You can also use this strategy if you have not been successful in getting items off your credit report using other methods, as opting to go the dispute way might only make the process cyclic, cumbersome, tiresome, and frustrating; you don't want to get into this cycle.

Now that you know when to use this method, understanding how the entire process works is very critical. To start with, ensure that you get an acceptance by writing if they agree to your times; don't pay without the letter! After you agree, allow about 45 days for the next credit report to be given to you by your credit monitoring service. These companies have the legal power to initiate the deletion process, so don't accept anything less, such as updating the balance; it is either a deletion or nothing. If they try to stall the process by saying that they cannot delete the problematic item from your credit report, mention that it will only take about 5 minutes for them to fill the Universal Data Form. Don't worry if one company seems not to agree with your terms since another one will probably show up and will gladly take the offer.

In any case, what do they have to gain if they keep your debt when you are willing to pay? Remember that the records will just be in your files for 7 years, and since 2 years are already past, these companies have no choice, otherwise, you can simply let the 7 years pass! However, don't use this as an excuse for not paying your debts, since the creditors can sue you to compel you to pay outstanding amounts. The aim of this process is to ensure that whatever bad experience you have with one creditor, doesn't make the others make unfavorable decisions on your part.

Note: Don't be overly aggressive with creditors who have a lot to lose in the process, especially the recent creditors, since they can probably sue you. Your goal is to only be aggressive with creditors that are barred by the statute of limitation from suing you in court. You don't want to find yourself in legal troubles to add to your existing problems. Try and remain as smart as possible and make all the right moves to help you repair your credit at the earliest.

Pay-to-delete isn't the only option available to you; you can use other strategies to repair your credit.

Check for FDCPA (Fair Debt Collection Practices Act) Violations

The law is very clear on what collection agencies can do and what they cannot do as far as debt collection is concerned. For instance:

- They should not call you more than once a day unless they can prove that it was accidentally dialed by their automated systems.
- They cannot call you before 8.00 am or after 9.00 pm.
- They cannot threaten, belittle or yell at you to make you pay any outstanding debts.
- They cannot tell anyone else other than your spouse why they are contacting you.
- The best way to go about this is to let them know that you are recording all their calls.
- They cannot take more money from your account than you have authorized if they do an ACH.
- They are also not allowed to send you collection letters if you have already sent them a cease-and-desist order.

If you can prove that collection companies are in violation of the law, you should file a complaint with the company and have your lawyer send proof indicating the violations; you can then request that any outstanding debt be forgiven. You need to understand that the law is on your side in such circumstances; actually, if the violations are major, the collection companies could be forced to pay fines of up to $10,000 for these violations.

So, if your debt is significantly lower than this, you could be on your way to having your debt cleared since these companies would rather pay your debt than pay the fine. Look for errors in your credit reports.

Your credit report should be free of errors. Even the slightest thing as reporting the wrong date of last activity on your credit report is enough to damage your credit. If the write-off date is different from what has been reported, you can dispute the entry to have it corrected to reflect the actual status of your credit. However, keep in mind that the CRAs will in most instances confirm that the negative entry is correct even if this is not the case, which means that they will not remove the erroneous item.

You must put in efforts to get them on the right track. To get them to comply, you have to inform them that the law requires them to have the preponderance of their systems in place to ensure that these errors do not arise. Therefore, the mere fact of confirming the initial error is not enough; inform them about the notice (summons) and complaint to let them understand that you are serious about the matter. Once they have an idea of your stance, they will put in efforts to do the right thing. The thing is that the CRAs don't want any case to go to court since this could ultimately provide proof that their systems are weak or flawed, which means that they will probably be in some bigger problems.

So, try and drive a strong point across so that they understand you mean business. The mere exchange of emails will not do, and you must send them details on how strong your case will be. This will make them understand their position, and they will decide to help you to avoid going to court. This will, in turn, work to your advantage in making them dig deeper into the issue. However, this method will only work if you are certain that an error was actually made. You will also require proof for it, so you cannot simply state that there was an error.

Request Proof of the Original Debt

If you are certain that the credit card has been written off for late payment, it is very likely that the carriers (Capital One and Citibank) cannot find the original billing statements within 30 days, which they are required by the law to respond to. This in effect allows you to have whatever entry you have disputed removed from the credit report as if it never happened.

Another handy approach is to request for the original contract that you signed to be provided to prove that you actually opened that particular credit card in the first instance. As you do this, don't just ask for "verification," since this just prompts the collection agency to "verify" that they received a request for collection on an account that has your name on it. Pay the original creditor.

When your debt is sold to collection agencies, you will probably risk having new items showing up on your credit report, which can further hurt your credit rating. However, you can stop that by sending a check with the full payment of any outstanding amount to the original creditor, after which you just send a proof of payment to that collection agency and any other then request them to delete any derogatory items, they have reported from your credit report.

Being in direct contact with your creditor or creditors is always a smart idea. In fact, many of these agencies will be fully equipped to cheat you and will follow through on plans to have your report show bad credit scores. It is up to you to try and remove these "middlemen" and do the payment yourself. You could also enter into an agreement to pay a portion of the money to the creditor as full payment for the sum (the pay to delete strategy).

Under federal law, if the original creditor accepts any payment as full payment for any outstanding debt, the collection agency has to remove whatever they have reported. This will only work if the original creditor accepts the payment; it is possible for some of the checks you pay to the original creditor to be returned to you.

Chapter 16.   Credit Repair Services

Credit repair agencies often make promises such as "you will be in debt" or "your credit will be restored quickly." However, they usually can't do anything more for you than you can do on your own, either with the help of someone else or on your own. Additionally, some of their promises might be impossible to keep. Let's take an example. A credit repair agency may argue that it will "remove this bankruptcy from your credit report"; while under Ontario law, bankruptcy can remain on your credit report for seven years. No one, not even a fee-based credit repair agency, can have the bankruptcy in question withdrawn before these seven years have elapsed.

Some credit repair agencies offer to improve your credit rating by giving you a loan that you would pay off over time. Beware: you might never see the money from such a loan, as these agencies use the loaned money to pay the fees, they charge you for this "service." Maintaining a good credit report is like presenting a beautiful school report to your parents: it gives you bargaining power to get what you want. Except that instead of having the right to take the minivan for the weekend, with the credit report, you can buy yourself one.

It is also a determining factor when shopping for a mortgage and financing. This can lead to a low-interest rate and optimal borrowing conditions. Also, some employers and homeowners will require it.

Since it is difficult to escape it, it is in your interest to pay attention to it. To finally understand how it works and knows the best tips for a file that will make you the darling of financial institutions, read on.

How does it work? Here are the essentials to enter the patent.

Periodically, lenders and service providers (cellular, internet, etc.) submit your account information (balances, payments, limits, open and close dates, terms, etc.) to Equifax and

TransUnion. These credit reporting agencies put it all together and give you a score ranging from 300 to 900, as well as a rating ranging from 1 to 9.

A high score indicates that you are in good financial health and that you can probably be trusted. I say "probably" because the credit report is not a perfect, omniscient tool. If you've owed your mom money since you bought her minivan in 2019, the agencies don't know.

The "1" rating means that an account is paid according to the terms. For each month of delay, the odds go up by one point to the maximum of "5" representing more than 120 days of arrears. An account sent to a collection agency or included in a bankruptcy is usually assigned a rating of "9." The rating "7" indicates that the account is the subject of a specific payment arrangement with a creditor.

Making the Best of Credit Bureaus

It is important to learn that all three credit bureaus have sensitive financial data. However, there is no method to prevent lenders and collection entities from sharing your information with the above companies. You can limit any possible problems associated with the credit bureaus by evaluating your credit reports annually and acting immediately in case you notice some errors. It is also good to monitor your credit cards and other open credit products to ensure that no one is misusing the accounts. If you have a card that you do not often use, sign up for alerts on that card so that you get notified if any transactions happen and regularly review statements for your active tickets. Next, if you notice any signs of fraud or theft, you can choose to place a credit freeze with the three credit bureaus and be diligent in tracking the activity of your credit card in the future.

The credit bureau company is also dominated by three major players as the rating agency, namely: Experian, Equifax, and TransUnion. A fascinating feature of the credit bureau's business model is the exchange of information. Banks, retailers, finance companies, and landlords send information to the credit bureaus for free, and then the credit bureaus contact them and sell consumer information back to them.

Credit bureaus are responsible for packaging and analyzing consumer credit reports obtained directly from credit scores. Unlike credit ratings issued in letters, credit scores have theirs issued in numbers, usually between 350–850. Your credit score affects the loan amounts you can pay for the debt and sometimes your rental and employment opportunities. You can access your credit report once a year from each credit bureau. Both rating agencies and credit bureaus are heavily regulated and have been under scrutiny since the Great Recession from 2007 to 2009.

How the Bureaus Get Their Information

To learn how the score gets calculated, we need to learn about all the different inputs of your score, aka where the bureaus get their info. You may have many factors that report information to the credit bureaus or none. Credit cards are called revolving accounts or revolving debt by the credit bureaus. Each month payments and balances are reported, as well as any late payments. This means that any cards that have your name on them will also report to all the bureaus. This includes cards that belong to a spouse or parent. Installment loans also report information to the credit bureaus. If you went down to your local Sears and financed a washer/dryer set by putting up a down payment, that is an installment loan. The details of these loans are all reported; the total balance, as well as the timeliness and amounts of your monthly payments. If you have mortgages or student loans, that information does get reported. Total amounts due, total paid so far, and the status of monthly payments is all reported. This information is kept track of and organized in their databases.

Chapter 17.   Your Financial Freedom

What is Financial Freedom?

Financial freedom is when you have enough money to live where, and how you want. It's having the financial capability to make any changes in life without the worry of debt. Ultimately, it's being able to do what you want in life without having to worry about the cost. This means that if an upcoming opportunity presents itself, like owning a vacation home with a friend or opening your own business, or even just wants a change in your lifestyle- you can do it!

What are some strategies for achieving Financial Freedom?

- If there is one thing we learned from our first strategy, it's that saving money is crucial. You must be able to save money in order to make it to financial freedom. There are plenty of ways of doing this while still being able to achieve that level of freedom you've always dreamed of.
- Setting a budget is key in attaining financial freedom. The best way we were able to set our budget was by dividing up the total amount we wanted into monthly installments that could not be exceeded. This allowed us to keep track of our finances so that we wouldn't be surprised at the end of each month but also it allowed us to enjoy some spending on things like movies, dinners, gifts, etc., throughout the month because those kinds of expenses are treated as luxuries.
- One of the biggest things you can do to reach your financial freedom is to invest. It's extremely easy for people to put off investing in their ventures for financial reasons, but it's very important that you put your hard-earned money into something that will earn profits for future use. It may be difficult at first, but if you stick with investing long enough, it will surely pay off.

Achieving a state of financial independence is the goal of many people. This means that they are no longer dependent on their income from a job. They have been able to build assets that generate an income, which may or may not be related to the current market, for their day-to-day living expenses.

The idea is so tantalizing because there is no limit to what can be accomplished with your time if you're not tied down by spending it just making enough money each day to live on.

4 Steps to Financial Independence

Financial independence is achieved in 4 steps:

1. You Should Have a Defined Spending Budget

When you have a concrete financial goal, you will be able to identify the limits of your income and be able to budget your money. You will then be able to analyze your spending patterns to determine where savings can be made. This could include cutting down on various expenses or making donations by refinancing your mortgage or purchasing an annuity from your company 401k retirement savings plan. The possibilities are endless and it's important to pick a spending goal that is realistic and within your ability to achieve within that time frame.

2. You Should Be Saving Regularly

One of the biggest complaints many people have is that they are not saving any money. If you've decided to go down this road, then it's important to practice saving regularly on a consistent basis. This can be done in a variety of ways. The most common way is a pay yourself first mentality, where each month you make a certain amount of money and allocate it into savings and investments. An example would be $500 per month in bonuses that are deposited into a savings account by the end of your monthly pay check. Other people prefer an automatic savings plan, where the money is deposited into the bank account automatically and then you have a portion of those funds set aside for investments. This can be done by having the funds go into an investment fund from your employer, or by putting it in an investment account on your own.

3. You Should Be Investing

This step is somewhat dependent on step 2 (solving your spending problem) as well as when you want to achieve independence. The idea here is to invest spare money that will not be needed until later in life so that when you finally reach financial independence, you will have something to work with. One of the best investment vehicles is a 401k retirement savings account. This is a separate account from your checking and savings accounts that you can contribute money to, withdraw funds from, and invest in a variety of stocks and mutual funds. It's also an excellent way to save for kids' college expenses as well.

4. You Should Be Living on Your Investment Income

Once you have built up some assets through investing and have a healthy amount of money in your retirement fund or future paychecks from bonuses or overtime pay, then you should be living off your investment income instead of taking any income just to make ends meet every month. This means you will no longer work for the financial security, but instead, your job will be to maintain your assets and perhaps grow them if you decide to invest in more income-generating assets.

These 4 steps are the 4 steps you need to follow if you want to achieve financial independence and not have a set of golden handcuffs holding you back from accomplishing great things in your life. If you're looking for something more concrete, than there is a neat little calculator that can help get an idea of how much money you will need at retirement to live off of based on how much income per month or year you want and from what age. It's called the Fidelity Retirement Income Calculator and you can get more information about it on their website if you're interested.

Chapter 18.   Mindset

Realization of Your Current Mindset

Before you start to make any changes, you need to know where your mindset is at the moment. Think of how you feel when you ponder about your credit card debt, as this will tell you more about your mindset than you might realize.

If you are like most people, you feel frustrated about your current situation. How you got into credit card debt will depend on what you are saying to yourself. For example, you might be angry or blame yourself for getting into debt. You might ask yourself why you allowed this situation to happen.

No matter what you notice about your current mindset, you need to accept it and understand why you feel this way. You also need to understand that it is okay for you to feel like this, as it will help you reach the get-out-of-debt mindset.

Debt Is Not a Burden but an Obstacle

There is a difference between a burden and an obstacle. When you have a burden, you have to deal with it; there is no way around it. However, there is a way around an obstacle. Therefore, you need to look at debt as an obstacle. It is something that you can overcome with the right steps. It is also something that you can keep yourself from getting into again.

Take a moment to think of ways that you can work toward erasing your credit card debt as an obstacle. For example, if you have a $75 minimum monthly payment that you have been doing, how much is going toward interest and fees? If you notice that this amount is $35, see what you can do in order to increase your monthly payment to $110. This will allow you to pay more than your minimum payment. More importantly, it will also allow you to put $75 toward your balance, with half of your amount toward fees and the other half toward your balance.

Don't Forget about Gratitude

Debt can cause us to become resentful. We often see other people enjoy the luxuries of life, whether it is by purchasing a new vehicle or going on a vacation. You might even feel resentful because they are able to afford new clothes. Allowing yourself to let go of your resentment and focusing on appreciation is one of the most effective strategies to break free from the negative mindset that comes with credit card debt.

Look around your home to see all the wonderful items that you own. Try to think about how lucky you are when it comes to your family, friends, and everyone else who is in your life. You don't always need to focus on the bigger things; sometimes, looking at the smaller moments is just as helpful. For example, you may feel gratitude when your child gives you a smile while they are playing quietly with their toys.

If you struggle with gratitude, one of the best techniques is writing down what you are grateful for at the end of every day. Find a journal and discuss everything that made you feel positive. You can also discuss what bad things happened, but try to find a way you can learn from them or turn them into something a little positive.

Take Responsibility for Your Debt

There is a big difference between blaming yourself for your credit card debt and taking responsibility for it. The biggest difference is what type of mindset you are in. For instance, if you are asking yourself how you could have been so dumb to allow yourself to obtain so many credit cards, you are blaming yourself for what happened. Instead, you need to take responsibility, which means you should try saying to yourself something like, "I know I got myself into credit card debt because I took out too many credit cards. Now, how can I start to pay off my credit card debt?"

Taking responsibility helps you have the right mindset because it helps you realize that even though you made a mistake, you understand the error and are ready to solve the problem. On top of this, you should always look at how you can keep yourself from making the same mistake again. No matter how you get yourself out of credit card debt, they are always going to be tempting.

Stop Seeing Debt-Free as a Solution to Your Problem

Another step you want to take to prepare yourself for your mindset of getting out of debt is to stop looking at becoming debt-free as the solution to your problem. The reality is that there is probably more than one reason why you are in debt. While you want to avoid blaming yourself, you also need to take responsibility for your mistakes.

Therefore, write down all the ways that you can become free of debt. This might mean that you should close all your credit cards and work on a plan to pay them off in a timely manner, or it may also mean that you should get a second job to help pay off your debt quickly. Instead of thinking about becoming debt-free as the only solution, you need to think of it as the outcome. You need to make becoming debt-free or having financial freedom be your ultimate goal. You should work on coming up with a series of steps that will help you reach your goal.

For example, let's assume that you're a college student who has opened up five credit cards. You are soon graduating and know that you need to start paying off all your smaller debts because you will be paying off student loans in the very near future. Therefore, you decide that one of your best options is to pay off your credit cards and no longer allow yourself to use them. Therefore, you work to think about how you can pay off your five credit cards in a single year.

Another example, you think about all the tips you receive from your job as a waitress. Typically, you bring home anywhere from $100 to $300, depending on the night and how busy it is. You realize that you can put all your tip money toward paying off your credit cards. This will allow you to pay off your debt faster. After doing the math, you realize that all your credit cards will be paid off in full by the time your student loans will begin requiring payment. Through your planning, you started to see becoming debt-free from credit cards as your outcome instead of your solution. By doing this, you were able to come up with a logical solution that works, provided that you are able to follow it over the course of the year.

Your Get-out-of-Debt Mindset

Set a Game Plan and Stick to It

You need to create goals and create your plan of action to get out of debt. While you don't have to write your plan down, this is always a good idea as it will help you remain focused on what you need to do. For example, you know that you have five credit cards that are all maxed out. In fact, you are close to going over the limit on most of them, which will make the credit card company charge you an over-the-limit fee. You realize that this will only create a larger amount of credit card debt. Therefore, you decide that you need to pay more than your minimum payment on these credit cards first.

Reframe Your Thoughts

Another major step for your mindset to get out of debt is to turn your negative thoughts into positive ones. This is one of the biggest reasons why you want to become grateful for what you have in life, including your credit card debt. Even though this might be hard to do right now, it is important to realize that this is a life lesson you are learning. In fact, by taking control of your credit card debt, you will be able to take control of your budget and reach financial freedom. Furthermore, the more negative you are, the less likely you will be to follow your goals and your budget.

Write down a List of Reasons to Get out of Debt

It will be difficult to get rid of credit card debt. In fact, you will need to take steps to keep yourself focused as there will be times when you will feel frustrated or will lack confidence in getting out of debt. One of the ways to overcome this is by writing down a list of reasons for wanting to get out of debt. This list can include anything that comes to your mind. For example, you might write that you want to own a home one day. You might also state that you want to be debt-free within two years. Another reason might be your children will be going to college starting in five years, and you want to be able to help them. It doesn't matter what your reasons are; what really matters is that they are your reasons for getting out of debt.

Realize that People Depend on You

If you have a family, you will want to think about all the people who depend on you for your income. It is a lot easier to be able to go out and buy diapers, groceries, and any other household items you need when you don't have to worry about what debt you are getting into. Instead, you can pay through your debit card or with cash without having to worry about the purchase again.

Set up Automatic Payments

Every credit card company's website will allow you to set up automatic payments. Some will even set up automatic payments while over the phone. Whatever you need to do, take time to set up these payments. This will help you make sure that these bills are getting paid. The trick is that you want to refrain from canceling or postponing your automatic payments, as this is typically an option. Again, this is something that you can put into your plan to become less likely to cancel the automatic payments.

Find Ways to Keep You Motivated

While you are creating your get-out-of-debt plan, you want to include ways that will help you stay motivated. Perhaps this means checking your progress every other month to see how much your credit card debt has gone down. For example, if you have five credit cards and you are paying $100 on them every month, you will see they have gone down close to $200 every two months. If you add this up, you have decreased your total credit card debt by $1,000. You can decide to track your progress through a spreadsheet on your computer or via a journal. Note the amount you owe when you pay and then notice the new amount the next time you make a payment.

Know that You Can Do It

Sometimes we struggle to follow through with our debt-free plan because we feel like we can't achieve it. It is important to note that there will be times you feel this way. There will be times when you feel unable to continue working on debt repayment. You might look and see that you still have two years of credit card debt to pay off and that your other bills continue to pile up.

Establish a Reward System

The fact is that you will find yourself struggling to maintain your mindset of getting out of debt from time to time. This might not be because you want to purchase something that you can't afford, but rather it may be because you find yourself getting tired of seeing how much money you owe toward credit cards.

Conclusion

Starting up a good credit score takes patience and some dedication. Always remember that it's better to do things the right way now than to have a huge debt or start over from scratch. With persistence, you can slowly rebuild your name with good credit down the line! Here are some final tips:

1) If you have asked for an extension on any payments during this time period, talk to the company or agency directly as people don't always communicate well when they're frustrated.

2) Have a friend or family member help you with keeping track of things, writing down statements and dates if something could have been misconstrued, or being supportive when you're upset.

3) Remember that you're the common denominator in any situation with bad credit. These things happen when people don't pay attention or make mistakes, but don't become bitter over something like this. It will only hurt your chances of fixing the situation and finding peace!

4) Look for possible errors on your credit report, whether it's a typo or an old job that has stopped posting due to the company being out of business. Make sure that your credit report is correct, and if you find something that's off, dispute it with the credit bureau. They'll investigate the issue on your behalf.

5) Work with creditors and credit reporting agencies to pay off debt or work out a payment plan. It might take time to settle everything out, but don't stop trying! The process might be more important than the result. If you break down the issues into smaller chunks of time, you can keep one step ahead of them instead of letting them crush your efforts over a period of years! Good luck!

6) Keep in mind that it's never too late to clean up a credit history. You'll need to work hard to make your credit score better, but it's not impossible with time and effort. That can be a good thing! It means you still have time to restore your credit history.

7) Take pride in the end result! You've worked hard to turn over a new leaf, and if you're happy with it, then that's fine by me!

8) If some of your credit information has been removed or there are mistakes on it, it's not too late to fix this! Make sure that the information is clearly and correctly noted. If there are errors or things that should be corrected, contact the company or agency for help with updating or fixing them. It will take time and patience, but make sure that you're working towards a better future.

9) With all of this in mind, now is a great time to start paying attention to small details. Keep track of your bills on time and don't let them pile up. All you have is your word...make your word good! If you take pride in doing the right thing, you'll be earning the best possible credit score down the line. Good luck, and happy chasing your dreams!

www.ingramcontent.com/pod-product-compliance
Lightning Source LLC
Chambersburg PA
CBHW081448220526
45466CB00008B/2551